Praise for *Dollcraft*

"There's no one else I would want to learn from or would trust more in this world or the spirit world than Patti. Her book is a guide to everything you could want to know or should know."

—ELTON CASTEE, paranormal investigator and YouTuber

"A fun and fascinating dive into the world of magical poppets and haunted dolls. … It's inspiring, easy to follow, and filled with Patti's signature warmth and wisdom. If you've ever wanted to explore the magick of poppets, this book is an absolute must-have!"

—PATTI STANGER, executive producer and star of Bravo's *Millionaire Matchmaker*

"I highly recommend this book for any doll enthusiasts out there! I have been a professional doll maker for over thirty-three years to the public, and a collector my whole life. … There are many secrets that us elders know that we can or cannot share all of the techniques, but Patti shares many in here."

—VOODOO QUEEN BLOODY MARY, artist, author, and curator of New Orleans Haunted Museum and Voodoo Spirit shop

"An essential manual for anyone venturing into the world of haunted dolls. . . . Patti leads the expedition into this largely uncharted territory with rare knowledge, wisdom, and first-hand experience. . . . What truly sets *Dollcraft* apart is her honest approach and ability to teach with clarity and heart."

—**DAVID L. SLOAN**, author and dolltender of Robert the Doll

"An insightful, exciting, and refreshing glimpse into the world of haunted dolls and magic poppets. Patti clearly knows her stuff; her knowledge of the subject provides readers with a unique opportunity to explore and experience haunted dolls and poppet magic for themselves."

—**FIONA DODWELL**, author of *A Cursed Book of Haunted Dolls*

"*Dollcraft* isn't just a fascinating how-to guide but is also a smart and entertaining look at the history and deeper meanings of dolls."

—**LISA MORTON**, host of the *Ghost Report* podcast and author of *Ghosts: A Haunted History*

"Patti's book will bring a touch of magic, motivating others to embark on their own haunted doll collecting adventures."

—**HALEY MICHELLE**, the Paranormal Princess

"This book will invigorate your senses and guide you to a high vibrational space and take you on the journey of playing along with the secret powers of Dollcraft on your own terms. This is a fun, essential, and exciting read."
—ALEX KAZEMI, author of *Pop Magick*

"Packed with poppet magick, haunted doll lore, and Patti's signature charm, this spellbinding guide is equal parts spooky and fabulous. Whether you're conjuring a protective poppet or channeling energy through a haunted heirloom, Patti makes it feel like a bewitching adventure."
—MICHAEL HERKES, author of *Glamstrology*

"Dollcraft is jam packed with interesting and important information. … This book uncovers the real truth and history of this fascinating topic."
—LILITH DORSEY, author of Water Magic

"As a clairvoyant who also collects haunted dolls, I'm so excited that Patti has created this wonderful book. I trust Patti's universal guidance and knowledge will help so many curious souls!"
—KELSI DAVIES, clairvoyant, actress, and creator

"Patti blends her lived experience, historical case studies, and practical magic prescriptions to handle and protect ourselves from haunted dolls.... This book breaks down how to create and infuse poppets with intention in a relatable and empowering way."

—CARDSY B, author, intuitive tarot reader, and wellness witch

"Patti guides the reader on an extraordinary journey into the bewitching world of haunted dolls and poppets, blending personal anecdotes, spellwork, and hands-on Witchcrafting with a flair only she can deliver.... Patti's genuine talent and pure heart leap forth from every page."

—CHRISTIAN DAY, author of The Witches' Book of the Dead

"Patti has given us all a veritable buffett of relevant and potent lore, practices, personal insights, and the wisdom that has been distilled from her years of research and direct magical and paranormal work."

—ORION FOXWOOD, witch, conjureman, and faery seer, author of *Fire in the Cauldron*

Dollcraft

Patti Negri

Dollcraft

A Witch's Guide to Poppet Magick & Haunted Dolls

LLEWELLYN
WOODBURY, MINNESOTA

First Edition
First Printing, 2025
Book design by Rordan Brasington
Cover design by Shannon McKuhen
Interior illustrations by Llewellyn Art Department

Library of Congress Cataloging-in-Publication Data (Pending)
ISBN: 978-0-7387-7748-1

Llewellyn Publications
A Division of Llewellyn Worldwide Ltd.
2143 Wooddale Drive
Woodbury, MN 55125-2989
www.llewellyn.com
Printed in the United States of America

Other Books by This Author

Old World Magick for the Modern World: Tips, Tricks, and Techniques to Balance, Empower, and Create a Life You Love

Acknowledgments

Writing this book has been a journey I couldn't have completed alone. First and foremost, I want to thank my amazing friend and producer, Christine Roth, whose encouragement and belief in my vision inspired me to bring this book to life. Your unwavering support and immense help from beginning to end made all the difference. I truly could not have done it without you.

To my editor and fellow doll enthusiast, Heather Greene, thank you for your keen insights and for helping shape this manuscript into its best possible form. Your expertise and patience were invaluable. I also want to thank my friend and producer, Rob Cohen, for his belief in me even when I doubted myself. Endless gratitude to my amazing husband, Kerry Crutchfield, for his patience and understanding of my endless hours sitting at my computer as he made dinner for me, walked the dog, and took care of our household. Your love and support have meant the world to me.

Finally, to my readers—this book exists because of you. Thank you for your interest, curiosity, and trust.

With Love and Magick,

Patti Negri

© photo by Dan Santoni. www.dansantoni.com

About the Author

Patti Negri, psychic-medium and "Good Witch," is best known for her recurring role on Travel Channel & Discovery Plus's *Ghost Adventures* and the hit YouTube series "TFIL Overnight" with Elton Castee. She is the international bestselling author of *Old World Magick for the Modern World: Tips, Tricks, and Techniques to Balance, Empower, and Create a Life You Love*.

Patti has appeared on numerous shows, including *Portals to Hell*, *MasterChef*, *Wipeout*, and *America's Got Talent*, as well as popular YouTube channels like Lilly Singh, LaurDIY, *Good Mythical Morning*, and *AwesomenessTV*.

She has been featured on magazine covers, contributed to over twenty books, and conducted séances for film, TV, and radio, working with stars like Emma Stone, Jon Voight, Josh Duhamel, Chevy Chase, and Gregory Hines.

She hosts the award-winning podcast *The Witching Hour* and co-hosts *The Witch's Movie Coven*. Patti is also a founding partner and Vice President of Paraflixx.com, as well as Headmistress and a founding partner of UniversityMagickus.com, an online school for spirituality and mysticism.

Contents

Part III: Poppet Spells and Recipes

Exercises

Disclaimer

While best efforts have been used in preparing this book, neither the author nor the publisher shall be held liable or responsible to any person or entity with respect to any loss or damages caused, or alleged to have been caused, directly or indirectly, by the information contained herein. Every situation is different, and the advice and strategies contained in this book may not be suitable for you.

In the following pages you will find recommendations for the use of certain herbs and essential oils. If you are allergic to any of these items, please refrain from use. Do your own research before using an essential oil. Each body reacts differently to herbs, essential oils, and other items, so results may vary person to person. Essential oils are potent; use care when handling them. Always dilute essential oils before placing them on your skin, and make sure to do a patch test on your skin before use. Never ingest essential oils. If you are allergic to any of the herbs or oils suggested in this book, please refrain from use.

Please note that the information in this book is not meant to diagnose, treat, prescribe, or substitute consultation with a licensed healthcare professional. This book is not intended to provide medical advice or to take the place of medical advice and treatment from your personal physician.

Readers are advised to consult their doctors or other qualified healthcare professionals regarding the treatment of their medical problems. Neither the publisher nor the author take any responsibility for possible consequences of any person reading or following the information in this book.

Foreword

The table was set, the food was served, and the guests were seated comfortably in their chairs. Planning this party had taken the better half of the morning, but now it was noon and everyone was happily gathered around my humble, yet welcoming, table.

As host, I lifted up my teacup to welcome my guests in proper fashion. I had chosen the Peter Rabbit china for this particular occasion, as it was spring and the Easter Bunny was everywhere. Before giving my speech, I paused to gaze at my guests. Teddy, my oldest friend, was to my right. Orange Blossom was to my left, with Cassandra next to her. Holly Hobbie sat opposite me, with Barbie (who insisted on wearing a hot pink disco dress) in her lap. Finally, there was Wilma Doreen, a timid-looking girl with blue eyes and dark orange hair made of yarn. She was the new doll on the block. I had just adopted her from the cabbage patch at Babyland General that December, and she still was not fully comfortable with this crowd. I gave her a small smile of reassurance and then announced the start of the meal.

We feasted on cookies and tea while discussing current events. I shared the latest lesson from *Schoolhouse Rock!* and they gushed about the roominess of their new toy chest. All in all, it was another successful tea party.

That was many moons ago, and some of those guests have moved on to other lives. Teddy is still with me, as are Wilma and Barbie (who is still proudly wearing the hot pink disco dress). All of my old friends are now showing their age, as am I, but they each contain energy from all our years of play as they help me tell the story of my life. That is what a doll is: a companion for a short time, or a friend for a lifetime.

Archaeologists have proven that dolls have been part of human culture for centuries. If dogs are humanity's best friend, dolls are a close second.

Whether a toy, a family heirloom, or a dust-collecting tchotchke, dolls have been an active part of our lives, unlike other manufactured, inanimate objects. Dolls will listen to our secrets and keep them. They will absorb family energy as they sit on a shelf, watching us come and go. They can remind us of who we are and tie us to our roots. And they themselves can harbor ancestral spirits and even help with our most complicated spells.

In this book, Patti Negri, a fellow witch and doll enthusiast, shares her passion for dolls and her experience working with them. I met Patti several years ago, and we immediately bonded over our shared love of dolls. We've compared our collections and even notes on poppet making. More importantly, Patti has taught me so much about haunted dolls through her extensive experience in the paranormal world.

Patti's magickal and spiritual talents emanate from a deep kindness and compassion, which allow her to intuitively access the subtle energies needed to work with magickal dolls. Energy and intuition, as she notes throughout this book, are keys to success in this work. Whether you make poppets or seek to live with a haunted doll, Patti will gently encourage you to trust your own intuition and magick.

I would encourage you to let go of any lingering fear of dolls and trust Patti's wisdom. Join her in this fantastic exploration of humanity's other best friend. You might find a powerful new magickal spell or two, or you might just find the next member of your family.

—Heather Greene

Witch, Editor, Journalist, and Author of *Lights, Camera, Witchcraft: A Critical History of Witches in American Film and Television*

Introduction

Imagine yourself surrounded by small faces, little humanlike beings looking back at you. That is the life I've lived for decades, and I do not teach kindergarten. Some of the faces I'm often surrounded by belong to the poppets I have created and used in my spellwork and my classroom. Others belong to the haunted dolls that have become part of my life's work as a psychic medium and witch. A few of these faces have even become my constant companions!

This book is an honest exploration of the practice of poppet creation and the related practice of keeping haunted dolls. From the many recipes for poppet creation, ingredients, and spells, to haunted doll facts and histories, to the details of hosting a Haunted Doll Tea Party or a funeral for a haunted doll, you'll find the essentials of doll-craft here.

My Love of Dolls

As a teacher of spellcraft, I work with poppets almost daily. One of the most popular classes at University Magickus, my online school, is the poppets class. And it's one of the most requested subjects I teach one-on-one in private lessons!

As a witch representing my practice on television, digital media, and audio—not to mention in my private consultations and my personal life—haunted dolls are everywhere I go. I've come to accept it. A few of them have even come home to live with me. But I must confess: I also happen to just love dolls. My living room is filled with non-haunted, non-poppet dolls; they're in my special collection and feature quite a few Barbies. These non-haunted dolls exist in perfect harmony with their haunted siblings and the poppets hanging out in my office.

The practice of owning a haunted doll appears to be gaining in popularity. In recent years, I've started to see more and more people showing off their haunted dolls on social media and in their homes. I've also visited amazing haunted doll displays in places such as Zak Bagans's The Haunted Museum in Las Vegas, Nevada; Bloody Mary's Haunted Museum in New Orleans, Louisiana; and The Warrens' Traveling Occult Museum in Monroe, Connecticut. More secretive esoterica practitioners may be unhappy to hear it, but popular culture has embraced the concept of haunted dolls, and their popularity shows no signs of waning. In fact, there are now haunted doll celebrities! These are haunted dolls with social media accounts and dolls that are profiled in books and movies, like the infamous Annabelle of *The Conjuring* and *Annabelle* movie franchises. Haunted dolls may have custodians or dolltenders, like Robert the Doll, who resides at the Fort East Martello Museum in Key West, Florida. Robert the Doll's dolltenders are the only people who handle him and travel with him for TV appearances.

My travels have led to some curious and marvelous encounters during appearances at conventions across the US and internationally. New doll owners (who range in age from preteen to senior) will bring their dolls with them, hoping for a quick consult. With so many sensationalized accounts out there, as well as a lack of information about haunted doll basics, it can be difficult for beginners to know which sources are misleading, exaggerated, or just wildly inaccurate.

As we enter a new era of enlightenment and self-expression, it's helpful to have a simple reference that cuts through the clutter and misinformation. That is why I wrote this book.

Defining a Doll

Along our journey, I'll answer the burning questions I get asked most often, such as "What is a poppet?" "What is a haunted doll?" and "How can you identify them?" First, let me start by defining the word *doll*. It may seem absurd to start a book about haunted dolls and poppets by defining what a doll is, but it is important to note that dolls come in many forms.

When someone says *doll*, they usually mean a child's play toy, but there is a universe filled with dolls of all shapes and sizes. A doll is a model of a human figure, and it is usually small, although dolls can vary drastically in size. Dolls can be made from practically anything that can be fashioned into a humanlike form, including the following materials.

- **Ceramic:** Classic antique dolls, porcelain and bisque porcelain; also called "china dolls" as a reference to fine ceramics rather than a nationality[1]
- **Cloth:** Rag dolls, such as Raggedy Ann dolls
- **Metal:** Nineteenth-century tin soldiers, for example
- **Paper:** Paper dolls were popular in the 1800s and 1900s[2]
- **Plastic or Mostly Plastic:** Barbie, action figures, Troll dolls, Lego people, Madame Alexander dolls, army men, etc.
- **Resin:** Ball-jointed fashion dolls, such as specialty anime dolls, and nineteenth-century antique dolls
- **Straw:** Traditional dolls from many cultures, often seen in museums

---

1. Giblin, "Kewpie Doll Charm Nears the Century Mark."
2. For more information, see Hosmer, "Hand-Made and Home-Made American Paper Dolls."

- **Vinyl:** Funko Pops, Bobbleheads, American Girl dolls, etc.
- **Wood:** Nutcrackers or wooden dolls, which are available at art supply stores in ball-jointed form or as eco-friendly toys
- **Yarn:** Handmade yarn dolls seen at craft fairs, on holiday trees, or at Girl Scout camps

This list is by no means exhaustive. You may encounter dolls (haunted or not) in your daily life and not even recognize them as dolls—they may be sitting on a coworker's desk or on a bookshelf at a relative's house. Think of the dolls you've seen either in person, online, or those that you've personally owned.

Now, think about a classic haunted doll. It's interesting to note that ceramic dolls are often the first thing that come to mind for people. These dolls can be off-putting because their hair is often real human hair or mohair, and they have a lifelike, painted face on the ceramic head. Ceramic dolls were popular throughout the Victorian era, from about 1860 to the 1920s, both in shiny porcelain and bisque porcelain. (*Bisque* just means unglazed porcelain.) With that being said, dolls of any material may be a vessel for a spirit.

Defining a Poppet

Poppets are dolls used specifically for magick and witchcraft. A poppet is a type of doll, though not all dolls are poppets. Poppets are generally homemade. If you fashion a humanlike figure from paper, wood, straw, cloth, or any other crafting material, it has the possibility of becoming either a toy or a tool for magick. It's all about your intent. If you cut out, hand sew, and stuff a felt gingerbread-man shape with the intent of giving it to a child as a toy, it's just a doll. If, however, you create the same form with the intent of using it in your spellwork, it's a doll *and* it's a poppet.[3]

If you have magickal intent, a poppet serves as the representation of a person. Poppets are potent tools for sympathetic magick, where the actions performed on the figure have a corresponding effect on the person or situation it represents. Sympathetic magick is based on the age-old principle of *like affects like*. The closer the connection between the poppet and the targeted person, the stronger your poppet's influence.

A poppet is a conduit for a range of intentions, including luck, love, wealth, health, success, and power, among many others. Poppets are sometimes associated with harmful or negative practices, such as curses or hurtful magick. However, in my experience, many modern witchcraft practitioners focus on positive intentions and ethical spellwork, a subject I will address in

---

3. I should note here that creating a doll as a toy is not the same as creating a haunted doll. This will be discussed in more detail in chapter 4.

chapter 9. Like any tool or symbol, the use of poppets in magick is highly dependent on the intention, beliefs, and practices of the individual.

Defining a Haunted Doll

Now, I'll contrast poppets and haunted dolls. While a poppet is a conduit for your intention and energy, a haunted doll can be thought of as a vessel, a containment for a spirit or disembodied energy. For the purposes of this book, I will define a haunted doll as a doll that is believed to be inhabited or influenced by a spirit, entity, or supernatural force. These dolls are often associated with paranormal phenomena, including reports of strange occurrences, unexplained movements, voices, or eerie sensations. As you'll read in chapter 1, the belief in haunted dolls is rooted in religion, paranormal folklore, and ghost stories.

Haunted dolls have many different creation stories, and like people, each one is unique. Their individual histories may depend on when the doll was made or where and in what culture the doll was made, not to mention the background of the spirit inhabiting the doll. Some are believed to be possessed by the spirits of deceased individuals, while others are thought to be vessels for malevolent entities or even the subject of a curse.

The stories and legends surrounding haunted dolls vary widely and can be reinterpreted or revised according to the culture, values, or beliefs surrounding the haunted doll, or even the individual tastes of the storyteller. Some accounts involve haunted dolls with unsettling appearances or a dark history, such as being associated with tragic events or past owners who experienced misfortune. These stories contribute to the belief that haunted dolls are imbued with a lingering negative spirit or energy. Other accounts tell of mischievous, curious, or mostly benign spirits.

For many, interactions with a haunted doll become their deepest connection with the paranormal. Paranormal activities are often attributed to the presence of a haunted doll's spirit or entity. These activities can include unexplained movements or changes in position, objects being displaced, mysterious sounds, or communication through electronic voice phenomenon (EVP) or automatic writing.

Why Dolls?

Many people ask why dolls seem to become haunted more frequently than other objects. Imagine being a disembodied spirit for a moment. If you were looking for a place to reside, what would be more fun: a stapler, or something with eyes, ears, a nose, and a mouth? Having eyes, ears, a nose, and a mouth would make things much more interesting, as you'd be able to communicate along the way.

Here are a few reasons I believe dolls are often associated with hauntings and paranormal activity.

Human Likeness and Anthropomorphism

Dolls are designed to resemble human beings, particularly in terms of their facial features, eyes, and limbs. It's only natural that this human likeness evokes a sense of familiarity and connection in people, leading us to assign emotions to the doll or at least open ourselves up to the possibility of a doll acting independently. When a doll is perceived as behaving in an unusual or unexpected manner, it can be particularly unsettling because it seems to blur the line between the inanimate and the living. The idea of a doll "coming to life" or being possessed by a spirit taps into primal fears and triggers the uncanny feeling of something being not quite right.

Symbolism and Beliefs

Dolls have held significant cultural and religious symbolism in almost every culture throughout history. In some belief systems, dolls have been used as vessels for spirits. In others, they have been employed in rituals and ceremonies to connect with the supernatural realm, from fertility rituals to funerary traditions. In the Shinto religion of Japan, special dolls called *hitogata* are sometimes used as vessels for spirits called *kami*. Dolls can provide a physical form for a spirit to aid in worship or communication. In animistic cultures, it's believed that spirits inhabit all objects, including dolls. That's the definition of *animism*. So, dolls can be used to communicate or to appease these spirits. These associations can create an underlying belief that dolls have a higher likelihood of being receptacles for spiritual or supernatural forces. The symbolic nature of dolls can amplify the perception of their potential to become haunted objects.

Childhood Attachment

Dolls often play a central role in childhood experiences. They can be cherished companions, confidants, and sources of comfort. As children, we may imbue our dolls with emotions, personalities, and even a sense of life. Children form relationships with dolls, having conversations with them, nurturing them, dressing them, acting out fantasies, and exploring their own emotions within the safe space of play. When a doll becomes associated with paranormal occurrences, it disrupts the innocent and nostalgic memories tied to childhood, intensifying the impact and leaving a lasting impression. The emotional attachment and vulnerability associated with childhood experiences can make encounters with haunted dolls particularly impactful.

Pop Culture's Influence

Popular culture has played a significant role in shaping society's perceptions of haunted dolls via movies, books, video games, and urban legends. Numerous horror films have featured dolls as central characters or themes, often portraying them as possessed, animated, or conduits for malevolent and murderous spirits. These fictional portrayals not only captivate the imagination, they also reinforce the idea that dolls are prone to hauntings. The influence of pop culture can contribute to the collective belief that dolls are associated with paranormal phenomena.

The Uncanny Valley Effect

Let's face it, some people are just weirded out by dolls. This may be attributable to the concept of the *uncanny valley*, referring to the psychological response people have when encountering objects or representations that closely resemble humans but fall short of perfect realism. Dolls have humanlike features but lack true life, which can often elicit a sense of unease or discomfort. The slight imperfections, glassy eyes, and frozen expressions can create an eerie or uncanny sensation, making dolls more susceptible to being perceived as haunted or possessing a hidden presence. That's probably why there are a lot more reports of haunted dolls than haunted teapots!

What's to Come

In part I, I will dive deeper into haunted dolls, discussing the dos and don'ts of acquiring and caring for haunted dolls along with the incredible backstory of this phenomena.

From a spiritual perspective, haunted dolls are believed to be vessels for residual energy, spiritual attachments, or portals for communication with the spirit world. Some people—including myself—believe that they can attune themselves to a doll's energy and access the wisdom or messages it may hold via deep meditation or energy work.

In addition to exploring communication with an already-haunted doll, I'll discuss the positives and perils of inviting a spirit into a doll, thereby creating your own haunted doll, as well as the implications of having an actively haunted doll in your life. I'll also outline the social activities you can attend with your doll, including doll funerals.

Part II of this book explains how to create poppets for spellwork, from materials to taglocking. I'll cover the benefits of constructing your own poppets, basic spellwork, and methods of empowering your poppet. I've also included descriptions of some of my favorite and most used taglocking herbs, stones, colors, sigils, and more.

Although poppets and dollcraft have been around for centuries, both are still extremely relevant today. In part III, I'll share a few spells and recipes for making your own poppets. I'll also teach you how they can be integrated into your current spellwork. You'll find instructions on how to use a poppet for healing, in binding rituals, and more.

Let's Begin!

This book is for beginners who need straightforward information as well as advanced practitioners looking for more insight into dollcraft, whether they are interested in poppets or haunted dolls.

This book is for the new witch who has learned all their poppet spellcraft on social media and needs a course correction. It is also for experienced spellcasters already well-versed in poppet creation who are looking to deepen their understanding of this vast area of magick. In fact, this book is for anyone looking to create effective poppets to manifest their intentions.

This book is for anyone seeking a better understanding of the world of haunted dolls. This book is also for those who have a real interest in working with haunted dolls, whether they identify as a witch or not. Because so many folks of all experience levels keep haunted dolls, I will cover the basics and provide advanced information about their creation, care, and feeding as well. I will by no means try to dissuade you from keeping haunted dolls. The practice of adopting a haunted companion is much more complex than collecting an uninhabited doll for anyone curious enough to engage in it.

I hope you find this book as much fun to read as it was to write. My dolls—haunted, poppet, and otherwise—bring me joy and inspiration every day. I hope yours will do so for you as well.

Part I
Haunted Dolls

CHAPTER 1

The Culture of Haunted Dolls

Why are so many people afraid of haunted dolls today? As stated in the introduction, some people find dolls disconcerting, but for others, there is a far deeper, more serious aversion. This fear is real. But it hasn't always been. In this chapter, I'll explore the cultural history of dolls and the fear that seems to be everywhere today.

Haunted Dolls Throughout History

Dolls inhabited by spirits or energies—good, evil, or neutral—have a long history across diverse cultures. Here are just a few examples.

Japan

One of the unifying ideas about haunted dolls across millennia is that they have either been created to be, or been made into, spiritual vessels. For instance, as early as the tenth century, there was a vast wealth of folklore surrounding *tsukumogami*, which were utilitarian household objects that were said to be granted a soul after one hundred years of service. These objects included pots, cups, musical instruments, tools, containers, and even dolls. After becoming ensouled, the tsukumogami were prone to tricking people. In one folktale, the spirits resented being neglected by their human masters after serving them for so long, and they become spiteful and murderous. After the tsukumogami wreaked havoc, they sought out a Buddhist priest, who began to teach them precepts. This eventually led to the spirits' enlightenment.

North America

Elemental spirits can inhabit doll-like figures crafted by Native peoples like the Hopi and Zuni. For the Hopi people, *katsinam* are benevolent spirits that surround them, both in the physical world and the supernatural or spiritual world. *Katsina* (also spelled *kachina*) spirits can bring abundance, favorable weather, and wellness if treated with respect. Dolls carved as representation of the katsinam are called *tithu* or *kachina dolls*. One of the earliest known kachina dolls was found on the Gila River; the doll was made of wood, and experts believe it was created around 1200 CE.[4]

Kachina dolls are not playthings, but prayer objects. They draw the spirit associated with them, as the spirit will be attracted to an image of

4. Wright, "Hopi Kachinas," 113.

itself. The dolls also serve as a reminder to respect the kachina spirits as family. Traditionally, men carve kachina dolls, with each doll serving as a representation of a specific spirit. Kachina dolls are always carved from the roots of cottonwood trees, an easy wood to work with. Cottonwood trees have special significance due to their water-seeking roots and association with water (and, thus, life). After a doll is complete, it is given to a girl or young woman in the village to connect them to the benefits the kachina can bring.

Central Africa

Spirits who can either act as divine protectors or wield the power of divine retribution inhabit the *nkisi nkondi*, literally "spirit hunters."[5] These vessels are created by Kongo sculptors. Nkisi nkondi are carved wooden figures empowered by the various materials placed inside them as well as the decorations done by a *nganga* (a spiritual specialist) on the figure's head, eyes, stomach, and back. After the figure has been made into a satisfactory vessel, a spirit is called in to protect, to heal, to uncover wrongdoing, and to punish oath breakers and practitioners of evil.

The process starts with the carving of a figurine. Though some figures may take the shape of an animal, human forms are the most common. The figure is then given to a nganga, who may place specific medicinal

---

5. Harris and Klemm, "Power Figure (*Nkisi Nkondi*), Kongo peoples."

or magickal herbs, glass, soil, nails, claws, or other objects into the figure and/or its cavities. Then, the nganga invites the spirit into the finished figure. Community members who seek advice or arbitration from a nkisi nkondi bring additional items to add to its exterior, such as cowrie shells, strips of cloth, twine, beads, pegs, and nails. Nails are a common addition to nkisi nkondi, as they are inserted to activate the spirit and request its help. With each addition to its exterior, the nkisi nkondi becomes more powerful. This practice dates as far back as the 1500s.

Ancient Egypt

For even earlier examples of spirit-inhabited dolls, look no further than ancient Egypt. Egyptians of high status in the Old Kingdom (circa 2700–2200 BCE), both noble and commoner, used *ka* figurines as vessels for themselves in the afterlife. These statues were so named because they were made to contain the *ka*, meaning spiritual aspect, of the deceased. Through the ka statues, the deceased could be animated by priestly spells to participate in funerary rituals.

Modern Fear of Dolls

Although enspirited dolls have been around for centuries, the fear of dolls is pervasive today. Currently, there are five categories of specific phobias in the *Diagnostic and Statistical Manual of Mental Disorders*: First, there are animal phobias (snakes, spiders, etc.)—you know, the friends who shriek if they see a snail. The second category is natural environment phobias, such as heights, water, or lightning. Following that is the third category: fear of blood, injections, or injury. This includes the fear of needles and the fear of medical procedures. The fourth category consists of situational phobias (i.e., enclosed spaces, crowds, or airplanes). Last is a catch-all category known as *Other*. That's where you can find a fear of clowns, fear of costumed characters, and fear of dolls.

Pediophobia

The intense, irrational fear of non-haunted, run-of-the-mill dolls is known as *pediophobia*. Like all phobias, it can induce excessive, persistent, unreasonable fear and crippling anxiety. While there's no specific phobia associated with haunted dolls, pediophobia coupled with phasmophobia, or the fear of the supernatural, sounds truly terrifying.

A couple of years ago, I was doing a séance around my dining room table. When I brought my haunted doll, Belle, into the room, one woman absolutely froze. She couldn't talk. She couldn't move. We all noticed the change in her immediately. When the woman could speak again, she said she'd had a dream just the night before where a doll that looked exactly like Belle was talking to her in her bedroom.

The woman was so shocked when I brought Belle into the room that she wanted to bolt out of her chair and leave. No matter how much I assured her that Belle was a good spirit and that the séance would be positive, the woman would not stay unless I put Belle in another room. I respected her wishes. Please remember to respect the wishes of anyone who wants to avoid a haunted doll.

Why Are People Fearful?

While dolls may have a higher association with hauntings in the collective consciousness, as noted in the introduction, this association ultimately stems from a combination of various psychological factors as well as an individual's cultural influences and personal experiences. These factors shape beliefs about dolls and similar inanimate objects.

It's also important to note that the very belief in the existence and validity of haunted dolls is also subject to personal belief and interpretation. Though it is common in modern times to encounter people who recoil at the thought of a haunted doll, this has not always been the case. In fact, haunted dolls and poppets have filled important roles in many cultures.

Here are some of the influences on both belief and fear.

Lifelike Without Being Alive

As mentioned in the introduction, dolls often possess expressive and recognizable features associated with living human beings, such as eyes, noses, mouths, lips, hands, feet, and even fingers and toes, yet they are not quite lifelike. This uncanny resemblance can trigger a sense of unease or discomfort in some individuals. The slight imperfections, fixed expressions, and artificial movements can create a feeling of something being "off" or unnatural, leading to fear or aversion. The very idea that a spirit *might* inhabit that "unnaturalness" is absolutely terrifying to those who have other associated fears.

Fear of the Unknown

Back to phasmophobia, the fear of the supernatural. Haunted dolls represent both the unknown *and* the supernatural. They blur the boundaries between the inanimate and the living, challenging our perception of reality. The idea that an object can harbor a malevolent spirit or possess a hidden presence taps into primal fears of the unexplainable.

Cultural and Media Influence

Frightening haunted dolls have become a trope in modern media—they're everywhere. Haunted dolls in popular culture have become sensationalized, leading to horrific, twisted, and terrifying tropes in horror movies, on social media, on television, in books, and via urban legends, reinforcing the association between haunted dolls and fear. Pervasive media depictions showcase dolls as demonically possessed, animated by evil spirits, or, at the very least, involved in sinister activities. The barrage of these portrayals in modern media have reinforced society's negative perception of haunted dolls and contributed to the fear and unease associated with them.

Childhood Associations

As mentioned previously, many people develop an emotional attachment to their childhood dolls, considering them companions or protectors. Fond memories of doll voices, playtime, hugs, and assigned personality traits created a deep, intimate, and special connection between a child and their plaything. Those with a fear of haunted dolls look at them as a betrayal of those earlier happier memories, seemingly corrupted by a perceived outside force. The disruption bleeds into the innocent and nostalgic associations tied to childhood. The collision of something familiar and comforting with the unknown or sinister intensifies fear and anxiety.

Supernatural Beliefs and Paranormal Experiences

For individuals who believe in and fear the binary existence of absolute good and absolute evil, or for those who have a sincere distrust of the supernatural, the idea of a haunted doll can be particularly distressing. These are people who perceive evil lurking around every corner. What could be worse than a childhood relic and symbol of innocence occupied by an outside force? Reports of paranormal encounters involving dolls, such as movements, changes in expression, or unexplained phenomena, contribute to the perception that dolls harbor not just energies, but malevolent and destructive energies. Reports of paranormal encounters contribute to this perception regardless of intent.

The Dangers of Haunted Dolls

Can a haunted doll be dangerous? This subject is often debated. Personally, I think haunted dolls can be dangerous. Peggy the Doll, for example, allegedly gave two people heart attacks.

I have seen dangerous haunted dolls firsthand. I had a problematic doll that was gifted to me by a friend; he had originally gotten the doll for himself. It was one of those little dolls typically sold in the French District of New Orleans as a memento; it had a wooden cross body, an oblong head with a painted-on face, and brightly colored feathers for hair. But after buying the doll, my friend realized he didn't like it—it was just too spooky, he said.

I happily took the doll in and kept it in my home office. It just sat there. For two years, everything was fine. Suddenly, I noticed that I no longer wanted to spend time in my office anymore. I had been picking up my laptop and working at the dining room table instead. I wanted to be anywhere *but* my office. I could not stay in my beautiful little workspace—a place I had always loved.

One day, I entered my office and looked around. I was drawn right to the little doll my friend had given me. I blurted, "Oh, it's you! I don't want you in my house. I don't want you in my office. You are negatively affecting my life, my home, and my work!"

I had to figure out what to do with the doll. I could, of course, banish the dark spirit—or I could get rid of the doll. Fortunately, I happen to know someone who really loves darkly haunted dolls and has the appropriate place to keep them: Zak Bagans. I had spent enough time with him (and in his haunted museum) to know that he would be the perfect person to adopt this little dolly.

I called Zak right away and let him know about the haunted doll. He asked, "Well, Patti, what is it? Show me a picture." When he saw the photos, Zak excitedly said, "Oh, it's a nail fetish hate doll. Yes, I want it." I immediately went to see him at his museum in Vegas and handed it over. He put it in a hallway cabinet near another New Orleans haunted object gifted to him by our mutual friend Bloody Mary. The day after I dropped the doll off, one of the museum's tour guides told me that it had started acting up that very first night.

The nail fetish hate doll had found its perfect and appropriate home in Zak's museum, a place where people go to experience haunted objects. It's well-curated like any good museum should be, but from a haunting and energetic perspective. The museum is like a roller coaster ride at an amusement park: it's wild enough to scare the pants off you, and while it might make you a little nauseous or dizzy, you know you are not going to die. Zak's museum is set up very much like that. Luckily, nobody has to live there.

Your home must be your sanctuary. It is no place for dangerous haunted dolls.

CHAPTER 2

My History with Haunted Dolls

As you've seen, haunted dolls have been around for a long time. They are currently everywhere we go—or should I say, everywhere *I* go. As a witch who has been involved in all forms of media, I encounter haunted dolls daily. In my work, I'm often introduced to them by their owners, and I am delighted to meet them all. Some of these dolls are famous. Some of them have come to live with me. Here are some of my stories.

My Own Dolls

I'm blessed to have been gifted a few amazing haunted dolls who have become part of my family. My favorite doll was sent to me by a complete stranger. Not all of them came to me with benign spirits, but with a little work, we've cleared bad spirits and built bonds of friendship.

Belle

My most adored haunted doll is Belle. She's an almost-110-year-old German doll.

Belle was sent to me by a woman in Belgium who saw me on the TV show *Deadly Possessions*, which was a spin-off of the show *Ghost Adventures*. In the episode the Belgian woman saw, I was doing a séance with another doll named Peggy, a notoriously haunted doll. (I'll tell you more about Peggy later in this chapter.) Because this woman had seen me with Peggy the Doll, she figured I could handle her own haunted doll, Belle.

The woman had owned Belle for three years, and she believed the doll had made both her and her toddler physically ill. She told me that Belle had even made her hair fall out. This is an example of just how negative haunted dolls can be, as discussed in chapter 1.

After the woman saw me handling Peggy the Doll, she contacted me and asked if she could send Belle to me. She wanted to get rid of the malevolent doll that had caused her and her family so much distress. I asked for photos and was surprised by what I saw: There was a good spirit in Belle hidden underneath the negative spirit.

When people ask me how I "see" spirits within a haunted doll, I can only explain that I see them intuitively. It's a vibration thing. Good spirits have a high vibration, and their energy feels light. Malevolent spirits have a low vibration, and their energy feels heavy. Belle's situation was different in that she had both. This is not something I encounter often: Belle was a vessel for both a negative spirit and a benevolent spirit being suppressed by the former. I needed to see Belle in person because I knew I could banish the negative spirit. So, Belle was packed up and sent to me via international post.

Although making live social media posts has become increasingly common in recent years, it was not common when I received Belle in this big box from Belgium (or, at least, the practice was uncommon for me). Suddenly, a brilliant idea popped into my head. *I should unbox her live on social media!* While I had never done a live social media event before, I was adamant, for some unknown reason, about documenting the opening of this big old box.

Looking back on this day, I'm now sure that it wasn't my idea—it was Belle's idea. The idea of doing a live stream unboxing of a haunted doll had never crossed my mind on a normal day. And yet, there I was slowly and carefully unpacking this well-wrapped haunted doll via Facebook Live as an ever-growing crowd tuned in.

Spirits have energy, and when that energy is focused, it is able to get the attention of any audience, even electronically. This energy was so powerful that fifty thousand people were watching me unwrap Belle on social media. I had followers in the tens of thousands at that time, but certainly not fifty thousand. The power of the spirit in the doll called the attention of the audience and drew them in. I have not had numbers like that on social media since—that's how strong Belle's presence was.

With everyone watching, I carefully unwrapped the bundle. Then I saw Belle. Her face was porcelain, and her arms and legs were made of composite, which is a mixture of wood, glue, sawdust, and corn starch. She was a beautiful doll. But when I looked at Belle, I felt her darkness. I felt her evil. I didn't know if it was a human spirit that was in her or something else. What I did know was that energy was not going to work in my household. I needed to act fast!

After logging off my Facebook Live and before sundown that same day, I worked with the newly unwrapped Belle to get rid of the negative spirit in her. I didn't want anything negative to escape at night while my husband, pets, and I were sleeping. Dark spirits are always going to go for the weakest, most vulnerable thing. For example, your pets or your children. This is why it is important to have a *positive* haunted doll. I did a complete banishing ceremony using protective herbs and crystals to remove the thick, dark energy attached to Belle.

I banished the dark spirit from Belle using the techniques found in chapter 6. While she seemed to be an empty vessel after I removed the dark spirit, I intuitively knew there was still a beautiful little spirit inside. The positive spirit inside of Belle had been suppressed for so long that it was hiding; coming out had to be on her timeline.

In the days that followed, I sat with Belle and got to know her. Even though the negative energy had been cleared, I noticed Belle was draining the energy of people around her. Even good haunted dolls have a bad habit of occasionally draining the energy of the people around them. Haunted objects—especially haunted dolls—will drain human energy just as much as any other kind of energy. They feed off of life force. Have you ever been in a haunted house and noticed that the battery on your cell phone drained super fast? Spirits can drain the batteries of flashlights, cell phones, and people.

In Belle's case, I noticed that people would come over and say things like, "Oh, what a cute doll!" A short time later, they'd say, "I'm so tired." While I was glad the negative spirit attached to Belle was gone, I didn't want her draining people's energy in my home. So, I helped make her comfortable. I kept protective objects around her for a long time. In particular, I kept a little satchel of rue attached to Belle's hand. Rue is one of my go-to herbs. The rue attached to Belle's hand kept her from draining everybody's energy and protected all the living entities in her presence. Over time, as Belle got accustomed to being in my house with all the activity, animals, and people, she didn't drain people's energy anymore.

As Belle slowly got more comfortable, her beautiful spirit started to emerge. At the same time, I noticed that my pets went from avoiding Belle to loving her. At first, my pets did not like Belle at all. Then, after everybody got comfortable and used to each other, my animals wanted to be around her all the time. My pets even brought her little toys and gifts! Petunia, my cat at the time, brought her a mouse toy, and Dora, my first dachshund, used to curl up by her. Belle truly became a member of our household.

Belle has the spirit of a little girl about six or seven years old. I think the girl had a sickly and short life, and her spirit went into the doll. Perhaps this was her doll, or maybe her spirit escaped into it—I'm not sure. In any case, now I have this beautiful little spirit that does not drain anyone's energy, and she is a part of my family.

Adopting a haunted doll really is like bringing in a new member of the family. But be careful who you bring in—make sure it's somebody you really want to live with. It is rare for a doll to immediately indicate that it is haunted by a negative spirit; you must figure it out for yourself. Dowsing rods, K2 meters, the Ovilus device, and various ghost-hunting technologies may help, but you yourself are the very best spirit radar. Trust your intuition, and trust your feelings as they communicate with you.

And remember, you can banish negative things, *and* you can call in positive things. I'll teach you how to do both later in this book.

Cheryl

Not all dolls are haunted, of course. I've got Cheryl, my non-haunted doll, in my office. She was sent to me by my friend named Cheryl, which is why

I named the doll Cheryl. She was to be Belle's little friend. Cheryl is beautiful, but she's not haunted.

One day, I was sitting at my desk teaching an online class, and Cheryl moved at least six inches across my desk. Both my hands were visible on screen, and nobody else was in the house. I didn't even notice it at the time because I was looking at my computer screen; my students brought it to my attention. Luckily, I had been recording the online class, so I was able to go back and look at the video footage. When I watched the video, I saw a large orb literally come out of my bookcase, go into the doll from the left side, move the doll, and then shoot out the other side of her.

I tried to recreate what happened, and I couldn't under any circumstances get Cheryl to move that smoothly. For a while, I was stumped as to how this happened, because Cheryl was not haunted. But a doll doesn't have to be haunted to be moving. It could be that another spirit was moving the doll. In this case, it may have been Belle playing with her dolly. Always research and investigate things as you go.

Baby Doll

I also have a baby doll. The doll looks a bit spooky because she looks so real. She was given to me by a friend who I was doing a house clearing for. The baby doll had a spirit in her that so bothered my friend that she said, "Just take her, just take her, just take her." I was happy to oblige!

But once I took the baby doll home, I realized she did not have a spirit in her anymore. I believe that when I cleared the house, I also cleared whatever spirit was in the doll. The spirit didn't stay with the woman who gave me the doll either—it was really gone with the clearing. Take that into consideration when you spiritually clear your home: Don't unintentionally clear wanted and beloved haunted objects!

The Nun

My trigger object doll is a haunted doll, but I did not know this until recently. First, let me start by explaining what a trigger object doll is and why this situation is peculiar.

While an increasing portion of the population is becoming interested in haunted dolls and poppets, it's important to differentiate between a haunted doll and a doll used as a trigger object. Trigger object dolls are used in paranormal investigations. They are doll "shells" built to house electronic ghost-hunting equipment like magnetometers, thermal sensors, or listening devices. They can be a useful tool for communicating with spirits, especially if the spirits are children or old-timers. Child spirits or spirits from days gone by might be frightened by high-tech plastic gadgets with bells and buzzers, but they are often drawn to a cute doll that has that same equipment hidden inside it. Trigger dolls are not haunted themselves. Well, usually.

I have a beautiful handmade trigger object doll of a nun. She seems to only light up when questions are posed about faith, religion, or spirituality; she doesn't work any other time. Recently, I was using this trigger doll with a good friend of mine who asked for advice about a certain situation. My nun doll lit up like a Christmas tree, and the spirit box sitting next to her said, "Pray." My friend had had a Catholic upbringing, and here was this nun doll telling her to pray. That was pretty cool.

Now, I am sensing an intelligent spirit living in (or hanging out in) my nun trigger doll. I do so much work in the spirit world and on the other side of the veil that this doesn't surprise me at all.

Famous Haunted Dolls

Some of my favorite haunted dolls are celebrities because of their positive and/or negative energies. Here are some examples of well-known haunted dolls that I've met.

Peggy the Doll

Peggy the Doll is my favorite famous haunted doll despite her negative energy. This is probably because of my direct relationship with her—and because I don't live with her. She is a cute little blonde doll that looks like the actress Doris Day. But Peggy the Doll has allegedly caused at least two people to have heart attacks, and she has made at least eighty people sick. Some of those people got sick just by looking at a picture or video of Peggy! Those affected experienced headaches, dizziness, fainting spells, heart attacks, vivid nightmares, or disturbing visions after encountering her.

When I first met Peggy, she belonged to a woman who was a paranormal investigator in England. I was there filming *Deadly Possessions*, Zak Bagans's *Ghost Adventures* spin-off. For the show, Zak brought together Peggy the Doll's owner and a young woman who had had a heart attack caused by Peggy. I was to perform a séance with them and the much-feared Peggy.

I was very cautious about what I said in front of Peggy on set. Spirits don't know the difference between video and real life, so you must always be careful about what you say. When the time came to do the séance with Peggy the Doll, I held her little plastic hand. All I could feel and sense was her darkness. She had some very heavy stuff inside of her. My goal was to get the young woman who had had a heart attack to confront Peggy the Doll and take her power back.

There are lots of ways to go about this. We did a beautiful cord-cutting ceremony with great success. (This cord-cutting ceremony can be found in chapter 6.) However, the type of ritual varies depending on an individual's belief system as well as the spirit or energy. For this ritual, I was not able to use the herbs and oils I typically use in my practice. However, intent and focus are always my main tools. I was also able to use my ritual knife, called an *athame*. A witch's athame separates energy, unlike a witch's wand, which directs energy.

During the ritual, I was able to energetically see the cords connecting Peggy the Doll to the young woman's heart. Using my athame, I literally cut through the energetic cords that bound them together. Next, I verbally and powerfully stated my intent out loud. The young woman and I followed up with some visualization. Without any other tools, rituals, or protocol, we were able to successfully protect ourselves from Peggy's negative affect and disconnect her from the young woman. Note that we did not take the evil out of Peggy; we just disconnected her from the young woman she had harmed.

Zak eventually purchased Peggy the Doll. She now lives in his haunted museum in Las Vegas. She's got her own room with other dolls, but she's the star. She has a spirit box that she supposedly speaks through. The tour guides at Zak's haunted museum let guests know that they're supposed to say hello to her; there's a protocol associated with visiting Peggy the Doll. Everybody wants to be respected, whether it's a spirit, a deity, or a haunted doll.

Thanks to Zak, Peggy the Doll now has lots of protective objects and spells around her that keep people safe—for the most part. Peggy still occasionally causes disturbances for some of her many visitors. When I visit, she just curses at me.

Robert the Doll

Another haunted celebrity doll is Robert the Doll. My good friend, author and paranormal historian David L. Sloan, is one of Robert the Doll's official dolltenders and often tells tales about him. David even wrote a book called, aptly, *Robert the Doll*.

Some believe that Robert the Doll is the inspiration for the *Chucky* movie and TV franchise, which is about a doll possessed by the ghost of a serial killer. However, Robert was not the inspiration for that franchise, according to his dolltender; David stated that Chucky was inspired by My Buddy Doll and blatant consumerism. Robert the Doll "originated around 1904. He was created by the Steiff company in Germany, and they're the people who invented the teddy bear."[6]

Robert the Doll contains both positive and negative energy, depending on who is experiencing him. In 1904, the doll was given to a young boy named Robert Eugene Otto; Robert Otto's grandfather had purchased it as a birthday gift for the boy when he was visiting Germany. The life-size cloth doll became a source of comfort for Robert Otto. He was named Robert as well, and he was dressed in a sailor suit originally worn by his owner, Robert Otto. As young Robert Otto became an old man, his attachment to the doll never ceased. After Robert Otto passed away, Robert the Doll started to

---

6. Negri, "Scared & Alone with Robert the Doll and David L. Sloan," 19:09–19:16.

act strangely. Those around the doll began to suspect that Robert the Doll was haunted by the spirit of the owner that had loved him.

Robert the Doll is displayed in a protective glass case—just the way he likes it—at the Fort East Martello Museum in Key West, Florida. Visitors have reported seeing Robert the Doll move and change expressions. They have also reported negative experiences to his dolltenders. The official website of Robert the Doll even features apology letters outlining ways visitors felt they may have disrespected the doll—including not asking permission to photograph him—because they felt cursed afterward!

Annabelle

The Annabelle doll has become incredibly famous due to its representations as the ultimate evil haunted doll in *The Conjuring* franchise and its films *Annabelle*, *Annabelle: Creation*, and *Annabelle Comes Home*. While in the movie, Annabelle is a scary bisque doll, the real Annabelle is a very ordinary Raggedy Ann doll made of cloth.

Here is the real story behind the Annabelle doll. A woman bought the doll in 1970 as a gift for her twenty-eight-year-old daughter named Donna. It was a birthday present. However, weird and unsettling things soon started to happen around the doll. Annabelle moved around the apartment. She also left messages for Donna on unfamiliar paper. Upon seeking the advice of a medium, Donna was told that the doll was inhabited by the spirit of a seven-year-old girl named Annabelle Higgins. This didn't feel right to Donna, who decided to look for more help after the doll tried to strangle her friend. Donna contacted Ed and Lorraine Warren, paranormal investigators who performed an unsuccessful exorcism on the doll. In the end, the Warrens took Annabelle the doll with them. According to the Warrens, the brakes and steering on the car gave out while driving Annabelle to their home.[7] Ed and Lorraine Warren eventually wrote a book about the events, which were far scarier than those depicted in the movies.

Now, Annabelle dwells in a special glass case in The Warrens' Traveling Occult Museum. Many people cannot make eye contact with the doll because they feel her energy so intensely. I have met Annabelle. In fact, another medium and I danced with Annabelle—or rather, in front of her case—at The Warrens' Seekers of the Supernatural Paracon in Gettysburg in 2024. The energy was real, and I was glad she remained in her glass display.

La Isla de las Muñecas (The Island of the Dolls)

Is there more than one haunted doll on *La Isla de las Muñecas*? It's extremely likely. This island is a creepy place. It is located in the Xochimilco canals near Mexico City, Mexico. The Xochimilco district is an amazing network of islands and canals, famous for its *chinampas* (floating gardens). However, La Isla de las Muñecas is famous for something else: it is covered with hun-

7. Eidell, "The Real-Life Story Behind Annabelle Is Even More Bone-Chilling Than the Movie."

dreds of creepy, decaying dolls that hang from the trees and are scattered across the landscape. La Isla de las Muñecas is now a peculiar and eerie tourist destination, and it's all because of a haunting voice heard by Don Julian Santana Barrera.

Don Julian Santana Barrera moved to an island off of Teshuilo Lake in the 1950s. Soon after he arrived, Barrera claimed that he heard the voice of a little girl calling to him from beyond the grave, saying, "I want my doll."[8] Legend had it that years earlier, the body of a drowned girl had washed up on the island, and it was followed by a doll. So, to appease the girl, Barrera hung a doll from a nearby tree.

Over time, Barrera believed that the doll moved locations from one tree to another. He believed that the doll was possessed by the girl's spirit and began collecting more dolls to appease her restless soul. Over time, Barrera amassed a vast collection of dolls, often trading them with locals or retrieving them from trash heaps. He hung the dolls, which were in various states of disrepair, all over the island, believing that they served as protectors against evil spirits and appeased the spirit of the drowned girl. In 2001, Barrera himself drowned in the canals at the age of eighty-six. He's buried on the island.

---

8. Atwal, "The Haunting Story of the Man Who Built the Island of the Dolls."

The legend grew, especially after Barrera's death. For the last few years, people have placed dolls that they claim are haunted on the island. Whether they are placed, hung, hammered, or destroyed, either whole or in parts, more dolls are finding their way to La Isla de las Muñecas every year.

Is the atmosphere unsettling? Of course it is. The atmosphere is intensified by this macabre art installation and dolls/doll parts swaying in the wind. Are the dolls on the island haunted? While some people believe the dolls are genuinely haunted or possess dark energies, others merely feel an overwhelming heaviness of emotion.

La Isla de las Muñecas is located at San Lorenzo Tlacoyucan, Xochimilco, 16043 Ciudad de Mexico, Mexico. Give yourself three or four hours to get there and explore.

Chapter 3

Your Haunted Doll

Do you want a haunted doll? Maybe you already have one. Or maybe you're not sure if your doll is haunted. Identifying whether a doll is haunted or not can be challenging, as it often involves subjective experiences and perceptions. A spirit may only give signs to you, it may only give signs to someone else and avoid you completely, or, as is the case with a doll of mine, it may only use the doll occasionally, entering the vessel to give a message of approval or disapproval about the activity in the household. The possibilities are dizzying and leave many in a state of uncertainty, questioning their own perception. In this chapter, I'll introduce the ways you can tell if a doll is haunted, whether it's one you own or one you encounter elsewhere. I will also share how to acquire one, if you don't have one already.

Do You Really Want a Haunted Doll?

First, you must ask yourself this question: Why do you want a haunted doll? If you are reading this book, you may already have a motive for wanting a haunted doll. There are lots of reasons people want haunted dolls. Examine yours.

- Does your reason have to do with a fascination for dolls and the desire to add a haunted doll to your collection?
- Are you obsessed with historical haunted dolls and want one of your own?
- Do you have a desire to use a doll to connect with the spirit world?
- Do you just want a roommate?

Whatever the reason, be clear and confident about your choice. If you are mindful, a haunted doll may present itself to you, as they have to me. Of course, you also have the option of creating or purchasing a haunted doll.

Signs of a Haunted Doll

You should always approach the identification of a haunted doll with a critical mindset and consider alternative explanations. Some signs, such as movements, could be attributed to natural factors like vibrations or changes in temperature. It is advisable to thoroughly research and investigate the doll's background, seek multiple accounts, and exercise discernment when assessing the haunted nature of a doll.

After you eliminate the ordinary, you can consider the extraordinary. There are several indicators that suggest a doll may be haunted. Here are some basic signs to look out for.

Unexplained Movements or Sounds

If the doll appears to move on its own, changes positions, or changes facial expressions without any obvious external cause, it could be a sign of haunting. Pay attention to any unexplained sounds coming from the doll or its vicinity, such as footsteps, laughter, or voices.

Energetic Sensations

Some people report feeling a distinct shift in energy when they are near a haunted doll. This may manifest as a sudden change in temperature, a tingling sensation, or a feeling of being watched or accompanied by a presence.

Anomalous Activity

Look for other paranormal phenomena occurring in the doll's presence, such as lights flickering, objects moving, or electrical devices malfunctioning without any discernible cause.

Emotional Reactions and Atmosphere

If being near a doll consistently evokes intense emotions, unease, or a sense of foreboding, it could be an indication of a haunted doll. Pay attention to the overall atmosphere in the room where the doll is located; some individuals report feeling a heavy or charged atmosphere when a haunted doll is present.

Reports of Paranormal Experiences

Gather information from previous owners or individuals who have interacted with the doll. If there are consistent reports of paranormal experiences, strange occurrences, or unexplained phenomena associated with the doll, it may be haunted.

Historical Background and Documentation

Investigate the doll's history and any documented stories or claims of haunting. If there are reputable sources or accounts supporting the haunted nature of the doll, it adds to the likelihood of it being haunted.

Animal Reactions

Check in with your animals. If you want to see if a doll is haunted, look at your cat, your dog, or your bird. (I don't know about fish.) How do they react around the doll? Animals can sense energy.

Dreams and Visions

Evaluate your dreams. Haunted dolls can affect your dreams and visions—for better or for worse. They act like batteries or conduits. It's great to keep a dream journal so you can analyze your dreams and reflect on them.

If you encounter a doll that exhibits signs of being haunted, it is essential to proceed with caution and respect. Treat the doll and its potential spirit with reverence. If the energy is too negative or if the work is beyond your knowledge base, consider seeking guidance from experienced paranormal investigators or spiritual practitioners who can provide further insight and assistance.

Buying a Haunted Doll

The benefit of buying a haunted doll is that it comes ready-made. You basically know what you are getting. Creating a haunted doll, which I will discuss in chapter 4, requires focus, ritual, and definite work on your part. If you don't feel confident in your ritual work or your creative ability, you might lean toward buying one.

Online

If you want to roll the dice when purchasing a haunted doll, you can look online. There are lots and lots of options. If you are getting a haunted doll online, be extra discerning. Don't trust what you read on auction sites or reports by similar sellers. If something seems too good to be true, it just might be a scam. Unfortunately, there are a lot of scammers out there who just want to make a quick buck off those looking for haunted dolls. The scammer will pick up a doll at a thrift store, create a haunted or spooky story about it, and sell it for a ridiculously high price to an unsuspecting buyer.

If you think you have found a reputable seller, do your research and read all of their reviews. If they've sold nine hundred haunted dolls, that's a bad sign. Assuming they were being truthful, no one has nine hundred haunted dolls unless they've really learned how to bring in a spirit—and if they don't do that work ethically or powerfully, they're going to bring in bad spirits.

Once, I was doing a house clearing for a YouTube influencer. She had bought a haunted doll online. It looked like it could have been a doll bought at any toy store; perhaps it was. The doll wore an African-print cloth dress and a matching head wrap. The seller said the doll was haunted, but to charge her, you had to do a spell. The spell came with herbs, oils, feathers, and a ritual to awaken the spirit in the doll. My client said she had never done the spell to charge the spirit, but there was absolutely no spirit in the "haunted" doll. It was just a little plastic doll with a nice outfit.

Yes, the spell could have called in a spirit. But I think it should have been sold as a non-haunted doll "vessel" that came with a spell to call in a spirit. Buyer beware.

Retail Stores

Another place to look for haunted dolls are major retail stores. These shops typically only sell spooky-looking dolls or dolls that look like haunted dolls from scary movies, like Chucky or Annabelle. In other words, they may *look* haunted but not *be* haunted.

Secondhand Stores

You will have better luck finding a haunted doll at an antique, secondhand, or thrift store. These stores are my personal favorites! Try going to the thrift store of your choice and just feeling it out. Trust your intuition. Perhaps you'll think something like, *I'm drawn to this little doll over here*. Many secondhand stores have a bin, a barrel, or a shelf full of dolls. Perhaps there's one in there that has a spirit! Trust yourself. Pick up the doll, hold it, and see how you are feeling.

My haunted doll Belle, discussed in chapter 2, was purchased at an antique store by her previous owner. The doll was over one hundred years old when she got her. This is one example of how antique stores and thrift stores are a really good way to find a haunted doll.

Assessing a Haunted Doll

Wherever you get a doll, whether it is in person or online, make sure to assess its energy. Ask yourself, *What does it feel like?* and trust your intuition. "Listen" to the doll.

Here are some general guidelines.

- **Trust Your Intuition:** If you have a strong sense of discomfort or unease around a particular doll, it's advisable to trust your instincts and maintain a safe distance.
- **Respectful Handling:** Treat the doll with respect and reverence, regardless of its alleged haunting. Avoid provoking or disrespecting the doll, as negative energy can potentially be attracted to or amplified by such actions.
- **Protective Measures:** Consider using spiritual or energetic protective measures—such as creating a protective circle, wearing protective crystals, or invoking a higher power—to create a sense of safety and establish boundaries. (I will talk more about protection in chapter 5.)

- **Seek Professional Assistance:** If you believe you are dealing with a genuinely dangerous or malevolent presence, it is recommended to seek guidance from experienced paranormal investigators, spiritual practitioners, or experts in the field who can assess the situation and provide appropriate advice or assistance.

Remember, the perception of danger associated with haunted dolls can vary greatly, and it is essential to approach the subject with an open mind and critical thinking skills. Personal safety is always the highest priority.

CHAPTER 4

Creating a Haunted Doll

If you don't own a haunted doll but have a doll you wish to enspirit, you can create one. Perhaps you could not find a haunted doll that already had a spirit, or a doll with a spirit you liked, or maybe you just don't trust online sellers. You *can* call in a spirit and create your own haunted doll.

It is important to note that intentionally creating a haunted doll is a complex and risky endeavor. Working with spirits requires deep respect, knowledge, and a strong ethical foundation. It is recommended to seek guidance from experienced practitioners, spiritual mentors, or paranormal experts who can provide further insight and support. Always prioritize the well-being and consent of all parties involved, including the spirit and those who may interact with the doll.

The Ethics of Inviting a Spirit into a Doll

Before beginning, you should review the ethical considerations of creating a haunted doll. It is essential to approach this subject responsibly and with respect for the spiritual realm and the potential consequences. Intentionally inviting spirits into dolls should be done with great care, consent, and a deep understanding of the potential implications involved.

Do not proceed with enspiriting your doll unless you can say all of the following with certainty.

- **"I have taken the time to thoroughly research and understand the history, cultural beliefs, and potential risks associated with haunted dolls."** This knowledge will help you approach the process with a deeper understanding.
- **"I have reflected on my intentions and motivations for creating a haunted doll."** Examine your reasons and ensure they align with ethical considerations, such as respecting the spirit realm and the potential consequences of your actions.
- **"I have engaged in respectful communication with the spiritual realm."** This can be done through prayer, meditation, or other spiritual practices that help establish a connection.
- **"I have sought permission and consent from the spirit I wish to invite into the doll."** Make it clear that the spirit has the freedom to

choose whether to associate with the doll. Respect the spirit's autonomy and do not coerce or force it into the doll.

- **"I have designed a ritual that I feel confident performing that is specifically tailored to invite the spirit into the doll."** The ritual, whether simple or elaborate, should create a sacred and respectful atmosphere.
- **"I am using elements that hold personal significance to me and the spirit I am inviting."** These items can include candles, incense, sacred symbols, etc.
- **"I will invoke the presence of the spirit, respectfully calling upon its energy and inviting it to inhabit the doll."** Clearly state your intentions, seeking permission and establishing boundaries during the ritual.

Choosing Your Vessel

Let's begin. The first thing you need is a doll.

Choosing a doll is an important first step in creating your own haunted doll. After all, this is a vessel for a spirit. The doll should fit your tastes while showing respect for the spirit you are calling into it. Some people like spooky-looking dolls, and if that's what you want, there are plenty to choose from at secondhand stores, as I mentioned in chapter 3.

You can, of course, spookify your haunted doll with paint and clothing. Adding dark circles under the doll's eyes and dressing it in tattered clothing can change its entire vibe. If you are talented at makeup, you can give the doll a more elaborate, face-painted look, which could be festive and spooky.

I prefer my dolls to be old but pretty—not spooky. My personal favorites are old or vintage dolls. Antique dolls, especially those from the 1800s and early 1900s that have bisque or resin heads and limbs with stuffed fabric bodies, look more like a doll that should be haunted. Plus, I think a pretty doll that moves unexpectedly is scarier than one that was made to look scary, but that's just my opinion.

The appearance of your doll can make a difference in perception, and your perception always affects your reality. Remember, your perception *is* the reality you live in, and your doll looking haunted will only add to your perception of it, along with your friends' and family's perceptions.

Even if it's not haunted, an older or used doll still has a history and life in it. I am an animist, which means I believe that everything has a spirit, not necessarily a ghost, but a distinct spiritual essence. A doll with a history will have more of an essence than a newer doll that has never been loved or played with. I believe that energy will add to the spirit you are calling in, both for you and for the spirit you are calling into the doll.

Another reason I like old dolls is because they are made of more natural materials. Before plastic was invented, dolls were made from ceramic, papier-mâché, wood, and other natural composites. However, spirits will certainly inhabit a well-chosen plastic doll. So again, it's all individual choice.

If you have a doll (new or old) with a specific cultural history, there is a chance you're going to attract a spirit with a similar cultural and/or historical background as the doll. For example, if you have an old doll from Japan, you might attract a Japanese spirit. Make sure you do your research on the cultural customs of the doll's nationality and time period to understand the possible motivations behind your haunted doll's actions. This also applies to extremely old dolls from Western European countries and early American dolls. It is not a bad idea to catch up on the culture's social mores and customs. If this ingratiates you to your doll, why not try it?

Preparing and Inviting a Spirit

After you have chosen your doll, you need to start the process of inviting a spirit into it. I suggest you work within your magickal path or spiritual belief system as much as possible.

If you are not an experienced magickal practitioner, I suggest you ask for help the first time. Perhaps begin the process with someone who is more experienced in magick and the paranormal. Ask someone with mediumship abilities or, at very least, really good intuition, someone who will have the ability to see or feel the spirits as they are coming in. This person will help you decide if you have called in a good or appropriate spirit before it takes residency.

Keep magickal ethics in mind as well. You only want to engage with spirits who *want* to be there. In other words, you don't want to have a relationship with somebody who doesn't want to have a relationship with you. The same is true of a haunted doll. You want to invite in a spirit that wants to be in that vessel. Who wants to be with you? So, consent is crucial, just like with humans.

Exercise
Preparing Your Doll and Inviting a Spirit

Before beginning, you must create your intent. This is very important. You will need to be clear about the kind of spirit you want to invite in. I cannot emphasize enough that you must request that only benevolent and good spirits are invited. These spirits make great haunted dolls, whereas malevolent or evil spirits just don't. If you have specific requests, like a young boy or girl spirit or an older, wise spirit, you will also need to state and claim that. Know your intent before starting.

Supplies

- Your chosen doll
- A sacred space to work your magick
- Your intent (please take this very seriously)

Directions

First, state that you are seeking a good, loving, and positive spirit that would like to inhabit your doll. State your intention aloud, because there is magick in sound itself. When you speak, you are using your breath, which is your pneuma, your life force.

Next, cleanse your doll. It is important to cleanse your doll so you are working with an energetic blank slate—no energies from its former life or its original maker. You can use any of the methods mentioned in chapter 5, or a cleansing method you normally work with.

Then, you will need to set up sacred space. Sacred space can be anywhere you have the privacy to create your magick, even if half an hour ago that space was the kitchen table where your kids had breakfast before heading to school. Turn your chosen space into a sacred place of magick and reverence. Creating a sacred space will both protect and enhance your magickal working.

To begin, make sure the space is clean, both literally and energetically. Light candles or incense, and gather magickal and ritual items you might work with. Then, create boundaries for your space. If you would like to cast a sacred circle or call the four corners, do so. If you work elementally, call the elements. Alternatively, say a prayer, chant, or do whatever works within your belief system.

Get yourself into a clear and connected headspace, perhaps via breathing techniques or meditation. If you work with certain guides or deities, invite them in and ask for their assistance and guidance.

Once the doll has been cleansed and the space is ready, it is time to call and invite in disembodied spirits. Say something like, "Who here in spirit would like to come into this doll right here?" State any requests, requirements, or boundaries that you have for the spirit in order to best fit your home and your lifestyle.

Now, this does not always work immediately. You may have to sit awhile. You may also have to repeat this ritual a few times until you find a spirit who wants to come in. When the spirit arrives, you'll sense and feel it. You will then have to see if it meets your requirements and if it's a spirit you want in your doll. Trust your intuition. Try not to overthink. If the spirit feels good or right, invite that spirit to stay in the doll. Welcome it into your home. Close the circle and your sacred space, thanking the spirits, guides, or deities who may have assisted you.

If the spirit feels wrong, negative, or just not quite right, thank it and send it away by verbally banishing it with words and intent. Be firm and direct. Say, "I command you to leave." Then, repeat the exercise, and ask questions and make requests with more specificity. Remember to speak with authority and confidence, without any anger or fear. Your intention is key.

Bonding and Protection

After a spirit has been invited into your doll, focus on building a bond and energetic connection with it. This can be achieved through practices such as meditation, visualization, or energetic attunement. In other words, spend time in quiet contemplation, holding and interacting with the doll. Develop a sense of connection and understanding with the spirit.

Remember to treat the doll with reverence and respect, seeing it as a vessel for the spirit's energy. Offer the doll a comfortable home and regular care.

Protect Yourself and Your Doll

If you are feeling drained in your daily life, it may be your newly haunted doll. Remember, even the best of spirits often drain our energy at first. Humans are the battery power they use to express themselves, move, etc. At this stage, it's important to familiarize yourself with the various protection techniques listed in chapter 5.

Protection is crucial until you get to know the spirit better *and* it gets to know you, the doll vessel, and its new home. Some people keep their haunted doll in a curio cabinet or glass case until they get to know it or while its energy drain is strong. Personally, I like to place the herb rue and leave a layer of salt or cascarilla powder around the doll. Similar protective elements, charms, or symbols can also protect you as you get to know the spirit.

In addition to protecting yourself, you also need to protect the spirit, because now the doll is a spirit vessel. You don't want something negative getting in. Create protection shields for your doll. Use prayers, mantras, invocations, smoke clearing, symbols, sigils, and protective crystals. Black stones are very protective, including my favorite: black tourmaline.

Establish Boundaries

Right away, give the doll explicit boundaries regarding how much it can do until you get to know it. Maintain very clear boundaries, just like with the people in your life. You can start by laying out your ground rules. Say the rules out loud—respectfully—to your haunted doll. Be prepared to repeat them. The firmer and more focused you are, the better the entity inhabiting your doll will understand you. You may enter a form of negotiation, like I did with Belle. For example, I told Belle, "You may sit closer, but behave yourself when I am in a live stream."

Once your haunted doll is settled and has its place, don't go to it for advice. The spirits inside haunted dolls are not high-vibration, unless you specifically called in a wise, high-vibration spirit. They're fun, and they can bring fun and excitement into your life, but don't make them into some wise deity.

As you get to know your haunted doll, pay close attention to your own moods, happiness, energy, and health. Haunted dolls can influence your life and your home in good and bad ways. If negative things start happening, including arguing, illness, and bad luck, you may need to rethink your new family member. If needed, you *can* banish a spirit if turns out to be negative; I will discuss this in chapter 6. Then, you can begin the process of looking for a new, positive spirit.

Establish a Bond

After a spirit has been invited in, focus on establishing a bond and energetic connection. Just like when you get a new pet or a new roommate, you must get to know each other. Getting to know your haunted doll may involve meditating near the doll, talking to the doll, or sitting and staring into the doll's eyes, if it has eyes.

As your doll starts coming to life, you will hear things like movement or even footsteps from the room where the doll is located. Their presence will be felt in the room very legitimately, and there will be no denying that you have a haunted doll.

Continue to always treat your haunted doll with reverence and respect. Offer it a dedicated space. Belle has made it known to me that she likes to sit right behind me while I work. She wanted to sit closer than I would let her, so she let me know she was there by pulling everyone's attention during classes, sessions, podcasts, and live streams. Ultimately, we compromised and met in the middle.

You are now responsible for the well-being of this haunted doll. Ensure your haunted doll is cared for and satisfied. Don't forget to regularly communicate with the spirit residing in your doll.

Chapter 5

The Nuts and Bolts of Protection

When working with haunted dolls or any objects believed to be inhabited by spirits—whether purchased, inherited, or created yourself—it is essential to prioritize your safety and well-being. Here are some quick protection techniques that can be used when dealing with haunted dolls. Note that these same methods can be adapted to protect your newly created doll from negative spirits. These protection techniques are meant to provide a sense of safety and maintain a positive energetic environment.

Energetic Boundaries

As outlined in chapter 4, it's important to have energetic boundaries to protect yourself and others from being drained or affected by your haunted doll. There are many methods to build those boundaries.

One simple way to do this is to begin by visualizing a protective energy shield around yourself before interacting with the doll. This shield acts as a barrier, preventing any negative or unwanted energies from affecting you. Then, set clear intentions that only positive and benevolent energies may enter your energetic space while working with the doll.

Exercise
Elemental Protection Spell

I like to use an elemental protection spell to set up my energetic boundaries. It relies on the four elements: earth, fire, water, and air. Here is my technique.

Supplies

- None

Directions

Center yourself and focus using slow, easy breathing.

When you are ready, face east. Say, "I call upon the east winds to cleanse and protect this space. May they bring me clarity and focus as they blow away anything negative or unwanted."

Face south. Say, "I call upon the fires of the south to burn away anything dark, negative, or unwanted. May they form a protective ring of fire around me, this space, and this working."

Next, face west. Say, "I call upon the waters of the west to cleanse and wash away anything negative or unwanted. May the mists of the ancestors protect me, this space, and this working."

Face north. Say, "I call upon the north and Mother Earth to wrap me in her arms of protection and keep me safe within her womb."

Sacred Space

You may want to create a sacred space to protect the doll from any outside influences from the spirit world and the mundane world. When creating a sacred space, first designate a specific working area or altar dedicated to the doll where you will conduct your interactions and rituals. This space can be temporary or permanent, depending on your practice and space allowance.

Cleanse the space regularly using methods such as smoke clearing, sprinkling salt, or placing protective crystals like black tourmaline or amethyst to ward off negative energies.

Protective Crystals and Amulets

A great method of protection is to place protective crystals or amulets near the doll, or to wear them as jewelry during your interactions. Crystals such as black tourmaline, obsidian, and amethyst are known for their protective properties.

Before using a crystal, you must spiritually cleanse it. You can, for example, leave the crystal in direct moonlight or smoke cleanse the crystal with palo santo or incense. There are other methods as well, including using water to cleanse the stone. However, some crystals cannot be cleansed with water. Research your stone before choosing a method.

After you cleanse your stone, you must charge it with its purpose by speaking your intent out loud while holding the stone. Then, the stone is ready.

Another method of protection is to utilize an amulet or charm that contains symbols of protection, such as the pentagram, a hamsa, or the Helm of Awe. Attach the protective symbol to you and/or the doll, or keep it nearby. My go-to symbol is the Helm of Awe; I use it on paranormal investigations or when I am deep in the otherworlds of any form. Cleanse and charge any amulet as you would a stone.

Prayers, Mantras, or Invocations

Add a layer of protection by invoking the presence of protective spiritual entities or deities that resonate with your belief system. You can start by requesting their assistance in maintaining a safe and positive environment while working with your haunted doll.

If you do not work with a deity, say a simple prayer or create a mantra that specifically focuses on protection and warding off negative energies. You can do this by repeating your desire for protection over and over. A simple mantra could be "Protect me. Protect my space. Protect the magick in this place."

Regular Cleansing and Clearing

Regular care is important. You can't just cleanse a doll once and then disregard cleansing forever. Engage in regular energetic cleansing rituals for your doll to remove any accumulated negative or stagnant energies. Effective methods include smoke cleansing with palo santo or incense, bathing the doll in moonlight, or using sound cleansing tools like singing bowls.

Be mindful of the doll's material before choosing a cleansing method. Some dolls, like composition dolls, cannot get wet. Some plastic dolls will melt in the sun. I also recommend choosing your smoke cleansing herbs carefully; I prefer palo santo or herbs with a mixture of mountain sage, sweet grass, rosemary, lavender, or other gentler ingredients.

After cleansing, remember to intentionally release any residual energy or attachments that may have accumulated during your interactions with the doll. Simply say out loud, "I release you." Sound itself is magick and will do the job.

Trusting Intuition and Awareness

With practice, you will develop a strong sense of intuition, and you will trust your instincts when working with haunted dolls. Pay attention to any feelings of discomfort or unease, as they may be signals of potential negative energies.

Be aware of any changes in your doll's behavior or energy as well as any changes in your own well-being. If you sense any harmful or malevolent energies, repeat the cleansing and protection techniques in this chapter. Do a cord cutting, if needed. If things still feel off, consider seeking professional help or discontinuing your interactions with the doll.

Chapter 6

Bad Spirits and Cursed Dolls

A cursed doll is not the same thing as a doll containing a negative spirit. A cursed doll is a haunted doll that is believed to be imbued with negative or malicious energy resulting from a curse or intentional malevolent intent. This is different from haunted dolls that contain an actual negative entity, like Peggy the Doll. Haunted dolls with negative spirits are also not necessarily the result of intentional acts.

In this chapter, I'll share a bit more about cursed dolls. I've also included two important rituals that will help you handle all types of negative haunted dolls.

More on the Cursed Doll

As I said earlier, a cursed doll is not the same thing as a negative haunted doll. Cursed dolls are also different from magickal poppets, where the figure itself is specifically created and then purposefully imbued with the intent of the person creating it. Cursed dolls are prefabricated, like other haunted dolls, and then are later cursed. A cursed doll is said to bring misfortune, bad luck, and even harm to those who encounter the doll or have it in their possession.

Cursed dolls can be created through various means, including:

- **Intentional Curses:** The doll may be the target of a deliberate curse cast by someone with the intent to cause harm or misfortune. This could involve rituals, spells, or specific incantations directed toward the doll.
- **Emotional Residue:** If a doll is associated with negative emotions, trauma, or tragic events, it is believed that the intense energy can imbue the doll with a curse. This can occur if the doll was present during significant incidents or absorbed the emotional energy of its previous owners.
- **Dark Rituals or Attachments:** Cursed dolls can be the result of dark rituals or practices performed by individuals seeking to bestow harmful energy or attach malevolent entities to the doll.

Like all haunted dolls, cursed dolls are often associated with eerie or paranormal occurrences, such as moving or changing positions on their own, causing disturbances in the environment, and affecting the emotional state of those around them. Some individuals claim to have experienced accidents, financial problems, or other misfortune after encountering a cursed doll. Because cursed dolls are rooted in folklore, paranormal beliefs, cultural superstitions, personal experiences, and supernatural legends, skeptics attribute any perceived negative effects to psychological factors, suggestion, or coincidence. Whether one believes in the existence of cursed dolls or not, it is advisable to approach them with caution and respect.

If you come across a doll that is rumored to be cursed, or if you feel uneasy in a doll's presence, it is generally recommended to maintain a respectful distance. Consider seeking guidance from experienced paranormal experts or spiritual practitioners who can provide further insight and assistance.

Cord Cutting

You may need to do a cord cutting to sever a negative connection between a haunted doll and a person (or persons). These ceremonies vary according to belief system; they can be simple or complex. A cord-cutting ceremony can take minutes or hours, but it is within your power to achieve. I will now share the cord-cutting ceremony that I used during my séance with Peggy the Doll.

Exercise
Cord-Cutting Ceremony

The following ceremony can be performed for someone who needs to be separated from a haunted doll or for yourself, if you need to sever your own bonds to a haunted doll. Personally, I prefer the buddy system. So, even if you are severing your own ties to a haunted doll, it's best to have a fellow magickal practitioner participating in the ceremony.

Please note that all the living souls psychically bound to the haunted doll in question must be willing participants. If they are against the cord cutting or if they are ambivalent, the ceremony may not work. Also noteworthy: The doll gets no say in the matter whatsoever.

Supplies

- A cutting tool like a witch's athame, a knife, a sword, or even a particularly sharp letter opener
- Protection ingredients such as salt, cascarilla, rue, dark stones such as black tourmaline, myrrh, or eucalyptus

Directions

First, protect yourself as a precaution, especially if you are unfamiliar with the doll. I recommend putting it in a glass case, if you can, and encircling the doll in some salt or cascarilla, which is powdered eggshell. My favorite additional tools are rue, which is a protective herb, and protective dark stones like black tourmaline. I often put oil containing a touch of eucalyptus or myrrh on the back of my neck for extra protection during the ceremony.

Next, get into the right head space to begin the ceremony. (This instruction applies for all participating in the ceremony, minus the doll.) Close your eyes. Take three deep, cleansing breaths in through the nose. Let them out through your mouth like a sigh. These exhales should be audible.

When you have finished, take a moment to center yourself or even recite your favorite prayer or chant. Because I am an elemental witch, I call on the elements of earth, fire, water, and air to aid me in my work using my favorite prayer.

Take a beat. Open your eyes. You are now in the proper mindset to make some magick.

Places everyone! Make sure the doll is away from the person who is energetically tied to it. There should be air between the two of them. That person should not be touching the doll. This distance helps you visualize the cords of energy between the two.

In your mind's eye, see the cords as they stretch through the air. There may be one cord that takes the form of a string, a rope, or a chain, or there may be multiple cords with multiple knots. The cord may even be a spiderweb! Follow the cord(s) to their end point, where they attach to each body: the person and the doll.

Ask the person who is with you to also visualize the cords.

Now, prepare for some cord cutting. Hold your blade and focus your intent. The blade is the conduit through which you will use your magick to slice through the cords. The person with you must also focus on the blade with the same intent. Remember, this will not work unless everyone wants these binding ties to be severed (with the exception of the doll, whose opinion does not matter here).

While being very mindful of your surroundings and the safety of others, slice down through the air where you visualize the psychic cords. The knife or blade will cut the energetic cords and attachments. Be precise; don't hack at the cords. Your intent is the knife's edge, and your focus dictates its sharpness. You have what it takes to cut through the psychic bonds. And be patient! Depending on how enmeshed the haunted doll and the person to whom they are bound are, the cutting step may take a while. However, you will eventually see the cord(s) fall away, disintegrating into nothingness. At that point, you have ceremonially cut the cords.

Next, state what you've just done, and state the intent that the doll's spirit will stay untethered from the person to whom it was tied. Say out loud in a clear and forceful voice, "I have cut the cords tying the spirit in this doll to [name]. They are no longer tied to the spirit in this doll." You can also add, "The spirit in this doll does not have permission to tie itself to [name] ever again."

Repeat this a few times. Be forceful. Being forceful is not the same as yelling—be direct, be confident, and maintain your focus.

Having successfully cut the cord(s), it's time to energetically end the ceremony. All participants (except for you-know-who) should close their eyes. Take three long, cleansing breaths in through the nose and out through the mouth. In through the nose, out through the mouth. In through the nose, out through the mouth.

Visualize all the negative energy and strife from the bonds, as well as your own weariness from the effort of cutting, all washing away. You are cleansed of this negative energy. The person bound to the doll is cleansed of negative energy. You can say this out loud: "I am free of negative energy." If you want to say a prayer or word of thanks, now is the time.

Participants can open their eyes. The cord-cutting ceremony is over. So mote it be.

Banishing a Curse or a Negative Spirit

Banishing a negative spirit or a malevolent curse from a doll is not like getting a stain out. This can be a complex and sensitive process. If you are unsure or uncomfortable performing a banishing yourself, I advise you to seek guidance from experienced practitioners, paranormal experts, or spiritual advisors who can provide further assistance and ensure the process is conducted safely and effectively.

Exercise
Banishing a Negative Spirit or Energy

In the absence of in-person guidance, I offer this exercise if you ever have to banish or remove a negative spirit without any outside help. Remember, to do so, you must approach the situation with caution and respect. You can't just scream "Get out!" In fact, evicting a spirit from its doll host when it does not want to leave can be an extraordinarily complex process. For that reason, I strongly suggest that you read this entire exercise before attempting anything. With that being said, here are the steps that can be taken to banish a negative spirit from a haunted doll.

Supplies

- Protective essential oils such as lavender, St. John's wort, or sage, either solo or in combination; you can also use a protective mix of oils found in a metaphysical store
- Several protective crystals to wear, such as black tourmaline, amethyst, smoky quartz, or hematite
- Other elements to protect your space, such as sacred symbols like the pentagram or Helm of Awe
- A sacred space for the work

- Salt or cascarilla
- Agents for spiritual cleansing of the doll such as palo santo, incense, salt, bells, or singing bowls

Preparation

Before beginning, you must choose a Rite of Release symbolic action, which is what I call the process taken to symbolically release the negative spirit from the doll. This will be done during the final rite, where you will focus on the actual release of the spirit from the doll.

The action you choose is entirely up to you. It's important to pick an action that is respectful of the negative spirit and that feels appropriate for your own spiritual practice. The Rite of Release can include one or more actions, from the simple (spoken affirmations, visualizations of the spirit's departure, etc.) to the more involved (placing the doll in running water, burying it in consecrated ground, etc.).

Whatever your Ritual of Release action happens to be, decide on it ahead of time, and be prepared to follow through.

Directions

First, set the intention that you are removing all negative, dark, evil, or low-vibration energies from your doll. Clearly establish your intention to remove the negative spirit from the doll and restore a sense of balance and harmony. Make sure your intentions come from a place of compassion, respect, and the highest good for all involved.

Remember, you are directing the spirit or energy to go somewhere else, somewhere it should want to go. Just saying "Go away" is not going to work—"away" is not a place. Instead, focus on a more positive plane of existence as the next destination for the negative spirit. Outdoors is a wonderful positive space where you could send energy or spirit; nature automatically transmutes.

Next, take the necessary protective measures. Wear or carry your protective crystal if you don't have it with you already. Then, grab your protective essential oil. While applying the oil on your skin, be mindful of any allergies. Always dilute essential oil with a carrier oil such as extra virgin olive oil before putting it on your skin; the usual ratio is two drops of essential oil to one teaspoon of carrier oil. Dot a bit of protective essential oil on the palms of your hands, the soles of your feet, and/or the back of your neck.

Next, create a sacred space by visualizing a protective energy shield around your workspace. (See chapter 5 for more ideas.) Consider placing a few more protective crystals or sacred symbols around your sacred space.

Then, put the doll in the center of your workspace and encircle it in some salt or cascarilla.

Invoke the presence of any protective spiritual entities or deities that resonate with your belief system to support you and guide you through this process. You can also invoke your higher self.

Now, you're ready to start the cleansing process. Begin with a thorough cleansing of both the doll and the space it occupies. Always check the doll's material before choosing a cleansing method. Use methods such as smoke cleansing with palo santo, sprinkling salt, bathing it in moonlight or saltwater, or performing a sound cleansing with bells or singing bowls.

As you cleanse, focus your intention on clearing away any negative or unwanted energies attached to the doll. Remain calm, respectful, and focused.

Next, engage the malevolent spirit within the doll in direct communication. Meditate on the doll and focus your intent internally. Then, speak your intent aloud. State in a firm but compassionate way that you are removing the negative spirit from the doll and guiding it toward a more positive and appropriate plane of existence.

Call upon a higher power or your higher self for assistance. You don't need to be religious to do this; higher powers can include benevolent spirits, guides, or divine energies. Seek their support and guidance in facilitating the spirit's departure from the doll and redirecting it toward a more suitable realm of existence.

Then, perform the final Rite of Release. You should have chosen your symbolic action by this point, and you should be prepared to follow through on the action you have chosen. Focus on your intent. Emphasize the importance of releasing any energetic attachments between the spirit and the doll, allowing both the spirit and the doll to move on from the encounter.

If you have followed the instructions successfully, the negative spirit should be released from the doll.

Removing Residual Energy

After the banishing ritual, you'll need to do one more round of energetic cleansing and protection to take care of residual energy in and around the doll. You can skip this step if you chose to bury the doll as your Rite of Release; the earth will do this final cleansing for you.

Once again, thoroughly cleanse and purify the doll using smoke cleansing, sound from a bell or singing bowl, or salt. Use your cleansing tool in the surrounding space as well, ensuring you have removed any residual negative energy.

Reinforce your protective measures with actions: Put protective stones around the doll, or apply protective oils directly to the doll to create a strong, positive energetic environment. Since the doll has been cleansed, you'll want to make sure that the doll remains free from negative influences.

Chapter 7

Living with a Haunted Doll

Most of the time, haunted dolls are fun. Like welcoming a new pet, you are bringing a living entity into your home. Think of it as bringing in a new family member to live with you.

There are many activities you can do with your haunted doll. A few of them will be discussed in this chapter.

Verifying Compatibility

However you choose to interact with your doll, you must prepare for your new guest and have some safety precautions in place. Instead of childproof cabinets and safety gates, you're putting up personal boundaries and protection spells. Remember, you're making room for another personality in your home. You've got to live with this other personality, so pains should be taken to make sure the doll you are dealing with is a match for the level of excitement in your home, is compatible with the environment, and has a personality that makes it a suitable family member. This kind of compatibility is the difference between a good fit for your haunted doll and one that does not add joy to your household and should be rehomed.

There are a multitude of haunted dolls that are positive in nature, and being the caregiver for haunted dolls that are positive and benevolent can be incredibly rewarding. A positive haunted doll will bring its unique personality, quirkiness, and sense of mischief into your home. It will bring positive paranormal activity rather than negative, scary paranormal activity.

This corporeal, three-dimensional world is humanity's realm of existence, so we have to keep an eye on any otherworldly things that enter—even those in our beautiful little dolls. No matter how wonderful and sweet your new doll is, you must remain in control. You are the boss. You can't let the doll take over, because this is your world, not theirs. When working with haunted dolls or any object believed to be inhabited by spirits, it is essential to prioritize your safety and well-being.

So, how do you know if your haunted doll is compatible with you? Ask yourself these simple questions.

- Is the doll making you sick?
- Do you feel attacked, physically or emotionally, when you are around the doll?

- Do you or others feel drained, emotionally or physically, around the doll?
- Do you feel angry, argumentative, or overcome with negative emotions when you are around the doll?
- Do you feel negativity coming from the doll?
- Do you feel calamity or bad luck associated with the doll?

If the answer to any of the previous questions is yes, do not bring this doll into your home. If you already have a doll like this in your home, you may want to consider a strategy to remove the negative energy or bad spirit from the doll, as I did with my doll Belle, or having a cord-cutting ceremony and rehoming the doll. Details about those rituals can be found in chapter 6.

The Haunted Doll Tea Party

There are many recreational activities that you can do or events you can attend with your haunted doll. Many haunted dolls have the perfect temperament to participate in group activities designed for both of you. Before doing so, you should know if your haunted doll is up for company. Do not bribe, cajole, or guilt your doll into participating in any activity. If they don't want to participate, it will not end well.

If you happen to have an outgoing haunted doll, it may attend a séance, paranormal convention, or other similar event with you. It may even interact with other haunted dolls. This brings me to a fairly new or resurgent type of event that you may have never attended: the haunted doll tea party.

Exercise
Hosting a Haunted Doll Tea Party

Hosting a haunted doll tea party may feel like revisiting childhood, or it may seem like something you would do at the American Girl café. However, this event is more like a mash-up between a séance and a group haunted doll interview. Think of this as a group chat for haunted dolls. Welcome to your new favorite pastime! Use your haunted doll tea party as an opportunity to connect with haunted dolls and their owners.

Supplies

- A venue (public or private) large enough for everyone to be seated around a table or tables
- Haunted doll(s)
- A group of willing participants
- Tea and teacups
- Sweet and salty snacks (for the living)

- Plates and other necessary place settings
- Ghost-hunting gear that is unobtrusive and can fit on the table

Preparation

First, create the atmosphere. Wherever you decide to hold your haunted doll tea party, whether it's in a public place or a private home, it is important to set up a protected sacred space. My favorite protection is the elemental protection spell (see chapter 5). However, any protection spell that reflects your intent to keep spirits within the room is appropriate. If you are hosting a picnic gathering, you may even consider a spiritual boundary: Visualize protective and uplifting white light around your table. Wherever you decide to host your tea party, do not forget to start with a protection ritual to set the tone.

The second step is to finalize the seating arrangement. Give your doll its own space. Seat the doll next to you. If you are bringing more than one haunted doll, ask them individually where they would care to sit. Ask your doll if it would like to sit next to another haunted doll; use your intuition to gauge the answer. If you are using a person-sized chair, seat your doll on a cushion or bring the doll's favorite chair to the event.

The third step is to consider tea and accoutrements. Start with something sweet, as you would at a séance. Who wouldn't like to start a meal with dessert? When making your selections, consider if your haunted doll seems to favor a certain scent, flavoring, or herb. Reflect that scent or flavor in the kinds of teas and scones, desserts, and sandwiches you serve. For example, if your doll likes roses, you could use rose tea. Maybe your doll likes lavender or lemon. You could provide lavender and lemon tarts or madeleines. Herbs like rosemary and thyme are also delicious in savory scones. Let your imagination run wild.

Research the herbs you are going to add to your tea and food selection, especially if you're unfamiliar with their properties. All of this is to say that you should let the (doll) guest list dictate the menu. And, of course, remember to reserve some treats for any dolltenders.

Now, you can figure out who you want to invite. I recommend you start with your favorite humans who might enjoy this fun and unique experience. Attendees can come with or without haunted doll companions. This gathering is open to all haunted doll enthusiasts.

What's important is not how many haunted dolls are in attendance, but that all humans attending are respectful of the haunted dolls. If there is more than one haunted doll, then you are in luck! If not, treat the haunted doll who attends like an invited guest.

Directions

Once everyone is present and seated, start pouring your tea. As a rule, haunted dolls generally do not eat or drink, but they may appreciate the offering set before them. Pour a cup of tea for their parents/dolltenders as well. If imbibing alcohol, keep your senses sharp by keeping drinking to a minimum.

Start by calling on all the spirits of the dolls attending to join the tea and conversation. They may not all choose to join you; accept and honor their choices, and encourage others to do the same. Leave the option open should the spirits decide to join you later in the meal.

Let the event foster deeper connections between owners and their dolls as they interact with others. Tell stories about each doll. Share your experiences. Both you and your human guests' psychic abilities are amplified in a group, as are your haunted dolls'. This is a remarkable opportunity to ask your doll questions. Bring out any ghost-hunting gear you have that is unobtrusive and will fit on the table. I'm talking cat balls, phone apps, dowsing rods, or possibly a portable theremin. You can also use tarot cards, a pendulum, or another divination tool. Leave the noisy spirit boxes and intrusive recording gear at home—this is a social event.

Document your tea party. Haunted dolls typically love photos, and photographs will often show orbs, shadows, or shapes not visible to the naked eye. And have fun with it! You never know what will pop up on a sound recording from your phone or on a quick picture or video. You are documenting a splendid occasion, and you never know what, or who, may show up.

Like a séance, end your haunted doll tea party with a salty snack. From sandwiches to pizza to pretzels, it all works. This is the end of the line of communication with the spirit world. You opened up a paranormal line of communication at the beginning of the tea party by calling the spirits in, and now you must close the door.

Thank the dolls, your human guests, and any other spirits in attendance for coming to the event, regardless of their behavior, and say your goodbyes. You are closing the door on this event and dissolving this link. Be firm; your spiritual guests will respect this and get the picture. Make sure of your guests' well-being (whether they are human or doll) and thank them for coming. This is some old-school etiquette, and it's just the kind that ensures there are no wayward spirits as a result of your shindig.

Incorporating Haunted Dolls into Spiritual Practices

If you want your doll to be part of your magickal or spiritual practice, put your doll on your altar alongside offerings, tools, or ancestral photographs. This is another good way to bond with your doll. If you want to consider them a special member of the family, keep them somewhere they can see and be a part of fun household interactions.

Haunted dolls can be incorporated into practices like divination by using them as focal points for scrying or as objects to receive messages or impressions. They can also be used in energy-healing practices by channeling healing energies through the doll.

I have occasionally used a trusted haunted doll in divination rituals. By holding the doll close and focusing my intentions, I was able to receive vivid visions and intuitive insights that guided me through a challenging situation. Remember, the wisdom is not coming from the doll, but from higher planes: your guides, your higher self, or a deity.

You can also use your haunted doll in a ritual to honor your ancestors. By including the doll, you may feel a stronger sense of presence and connection to your lineage, particularly if the doll was owned by an ancestor. Incorporating a haunted doll in this way can facilitate a deep and meaningful experience.

Hosting a Funeral for a Doll

What if you don't want your haunted doll anymore? Maybe you had children or experienced a lifestyle change, or maybe you are just too busy with other things to take on the responsibility of having a haunted doll. Remember, there are two parts to your doll: the physical doll itself (the vessel) and the spirit that resides in it. The spirit is the most important part.

If the spirit is happy being in the doll, I would try to find a new person to give or sell the doll to. Especially considering the popularity of and desire for haunted dolls right now, your doll could be quite the commodity! Personally, I would make sure the person is a worthy keeper for the doll and is not planning to torture it or harm the spirit. Rehoming your doll should be given the same care and dedication as rehoming a beloved pet. Do make sure that the person knows the doll is haunted; don't just give it away. If you would rather donate the doll to a thrift store or something, you should add a note about the spirit in the doll. Another good option is to gift your haunted doll to a professional paranormal investigator, witch, or museum.

If for some reason the spirit is *not* happy being in the doll—and believe me, you will know—do a releasing ceremony for the spirit. Invite it to leave its doll vessel if it so desires. Then, you can get rid of the vessel. Trust your intuition.

A Beautiful Doll Life

Haunted dolls can be a beautiful addition to your life, to your home, and even to your magickal or spiritual practice, if you so desire. Within these dolls lies an opportunity for deeper understanding and acceptance of the unknown. Haunted dolls become mirrors for exploring our own fears, confronting the shadows within us, and ultimately embracing compassion and healing. May this inspire you to perceive haunted dolls not solely as sources of excitement or terror, but as gateways to self-discovery and empathy. Find solace in the profound mysteries life offers.

Part II
Poppet Magick

Chapter 8

The Culture of Poppets

As stated at the beginning of this book, poppets are dolls used in folk magick and witchcraft. A poppet is a doll made to represent a person in order to cast spells for good or evil purposes, or to magickally aid a person in luck, love, or healing. Poppets can also be used in spells or rituals to attract or influence an outcome for a group, such as a positive outcome for a game or a battle. Here are some hypotheticals: Hunters may create a poppet for good luck on their expeditions. Those who are forever at odds with their neighbors may create a binding poppet to help end the strife. A group of people who are being oppressed could create a much-needed protection poppet. A football fan who really wants their favorite player to do well in a game could charge a luck poppet to help them to victory. Poppet usage depends on what is needed at the time.

Like haunted dolls, poppets have their presence steeped in folklore and cultural and historical significance. From the Jewish legend of the golem to the pop culture representations of "voodoo dolls," poppets of all kinds have long occupied our imaginations. However, as opposed to a haunted doll, which is a vessel for an external spirit, a poppet is a tool you create and imbue with your intent.

A poppet's use is dictated by the cultural, historical, and societal priorities of the person or group using it. It's all about time and place.

Poppet History

Cultures across history have created and charged figures for their most pressing problems: hunting, the harvest, fertility, protection, etc. The oldest discovered figure is known as *Löwenmensch*, or the Lion Man. It was discovered in a cave located in a cliff in southern Germany. Experts estimate the figure is forty thousand years old. The figure is about twelve inches tall and is carved of mammoth tusk ivory. It has a feline head. The carving of the figurine took time; it's intricate, and it took skill. Yet it seems to hold no value as an Ice Age tool. According to scholars, "The wear on his body caused by handling suggests that he was passed around and rubbed as part of a narrative or ritual that would explain his appearance and meaning."[9] So, what was its purpose? Could it have been used as a poppet? Could it have been used by those hoping to exhibit leonine skill while hunting?

9. Cook, "The Lion Man."

Imagine any of the two hundred or so Venus figurines found across Eurasia that date from the Gravettian Period, around thirty thousand years ago. These faceless figures often had large breasts, hips, and bellies, with many scholars theorizing they were fertility figures, effectively making them poppets for sexual fertility or abundance. Like the Löwenmensch, we can't definitively say how they were used, but researchers believe there were likely many uses based on differences in design, posture, and the location where they were found.[10]

When we fast-forward several thousand years, both the magick and intent of poppet magick becomes more complex. About four thousand years ago, the Egyptians of the mid-Twelfth and early Thirteenth Dynasties believed in the power of sympathetic magick, where creating a representation of a person or object could influence the real thing. These poppets, also known as execration figurines, were used against adversaries (including foreign places, rulers, and/or individual enemies) by writing names directly on the figurines. The figurines were portrayed as bound and terrified for good measure. They were then smashed as a symbol of the enemy's defeat.

In ancient Greek writings, figurines known as *kolossoi* were made of wax or wood. Kolossoi were used in protection, binding, and erotic

10. Hyland, "The Well-Dressed Venus," 7.

magick. They also had other uses. A fourth-century inscription detailed that early Greek settlers took an oath to not abandon their settlement in Cyrene, Libya. When the oath was broken, wax kolossoi were made, and men, women, and children then tossed the wax figurines into a fire. As the figures burned, all gathered "to pronounce a curse that those who had not remained true to the oaths were to melt away and dissolve like the *kolossoi* along with their offspring and their goods."[11]

My favorite historical poppets are those steeped in folklore, such as the golem of Jewish folklore. A literal poppet formed out of mud or clay, a golem was formed to do its maker's bidding. Golems possessed no free will because they were made by man, not by God. Often, golems were asked to protect the Jewish people. In the 1500s, a legend sprang up about a Polish rabbi, Elijah Ba'al Shem, who wrote *emet* ("truth") on a sign and hung it on a figure. (Some versions of the story have the word written on the figure's forehead.) To his surprise, the figure sprang to life! When the sign was removed, the figure disintegrated back into dust.

When you embark on your own exploration of poppet magick, you are following a tradition that has been around for thousands of years.

---

11. Dickie, "What Is a *Kolossos* and How Were *Kolossoi* Made in the Hellenistic Period?" 237.

Poppet Principles

While the complexity of the ideas behind poppet magick may have changed over time, all poppet usage relies on the same principles. A magickal practitioner creates a poppet with magickal intent. Then, the practitioner charges the doll with a spell for the desired outcome. In your practice, the meaning and significance of poppets ultimately depends on your individual beliefs and practices. You can think of the historical and cultural uses of poppets as building blocks in the story of your modern poppet's spell.

Poppets typically represent the individual to whom the magick or intent is being directed. The process uses sympathetic magick and involves the performance of a ritual using a magickal object, like the poppets you will create, to influence either an event or a person. This person can be a loved one, someone you barely know, a group, or even yourself. When you make a poppet, you are creating an object that has been a staple of sympathetic magick for generations.

You can make poppets out of just about anything. They can be as complex or as simple as you have the time and patience for. A poppet's appearance can be as realistic or as abstract as you would like; all that matters is that it is recognizable to you. Some people sew faces on their poppets, while others make fast, easy faces with a Sharpie. There is no grade on this art project! If you would prefer not to customize your poppet, the only tools you technically need are your imagination and intent.

Many people I encounter wonder how or when to use a poppet in spellwork. Poppets are powerful tools in modern magick because in addition to giving you something tangible to work with, they are great for remote work, including distance healing. In the era of video calls, social media, and long-distance friendships, what could be more fitting? Poppets are also terrific for self-care and empowerment. You can give your poppet a face and body that represents you, then work with that poppet and/or put it on your altar.

Despite pop culture's negative representations of poppets as agents of evil, poppets have been and are used for many beneficial purposes, from healing, love, luck, and prosperity to the necessary protections of binding, banishing, and neutralizing bad intention. Here are a few categories of positive spellwork where the addition of a poppet can be a powerful tool.

Healing and Wellness Spells

Poppets are frequently used in healing spells to address physical, emotional, or spiritual ailments. You may perform actions on the poppet that symbolize the desired outcome, such as sewing up a wound, adding herbs or crystals for healing, or soothing the doll with essential oils or sacred waters. These actions are believed to influence the corresponding person's well-being and promote healing.

Protection and Warding Rituals

Poppets can be utilized for protection and warding purposes. Protective herbs, symbols, or objects can be incorporated into the poppet to create a potent shield against negative energies or harmful influences. For example, small charms or crystals can be inserted into or attached to the poppet. The poppet is then manipulated or treated in ways that symbolically strengthen the protective barrier around the person it represents.

Love and Attraction Spells

Poppets are often used in spells and rituals to attract or influence love or romantic connections. The poppet may be personalized with items associated with the desired person, such as a lock of hair or a piece of clothing. The practitioner may perform actions on the poppet that symbolize the strengthening of a romantic bond or the attraction of a specific individual.

It's important to note that ethical considerations should always be kept in mind when performing spells, particularly love spells. Respect the free will and consent of all involved. I do not advise controlling other people without their permission.

Binding or Banishing Spells

Poppets can be employed in binding or banishing rituals to restrict or remove unwanted influences or individuals from one's life. The poppet is used to symbolize the person or situation to be bound or banished. Actions performed on the poppet, such as tying it with cords or writing the name of a person to be banished, can effectively limit the person or situation's influence, or even remove them from your life.

Intention Amplification and Energy Work

Poppets can also serve as focal points for energy work or intention amplification. They can be used in rituals to concentrate and direct your energy, allowing you to channel your intentions and desires into the poppet. In this case, the poppet represents you. By visualizing or stating your intentions while interacting with the poppet, you can amplify the energy and manifestation of your own desires.

CHAPTER 9

Creating Your Poppet

Although poppet work is an ancient tradition, it's still extremely relevant today. In the next few chapters, I'll dive into the rich and exciting world of creating and using poppets in spellwork, healing, binding rituals, and more. First, here's an outline of how poppet magick works.

The Basic Idea

Your intention is the most important step in creating a poppet. First, ask yourself, *What is my goal?*

Once you have an intention, the second step is to translate that intention into action through the creation of the poppet. This act should be something you enjoy or at least feel confident doing. You should be able to develop a flow of your intentional magick to the materials. Poppet creation is a meditative, tactile experience. Don't be intimidated if you aren't crafty. When creating your poppet, you can use a pattern or just wing it. I'll get more into the art part later in the chapter.

Your poppet, much like a doll, can be made from any material you can craft into a figure, including but not limited to cloth, wax, clay, paper, wood, rope, straw, herbs, flowers, bits of plastic, or even premade dough from the supermarket. In short, anything you can craft with can be made into a poppet. Your creation can be made to last minutes or a lifetime. As you craft your poppet, your magickal goal becomes focused with the power of personalization. Personalization in poppet creation strengthens the energetic link between the poppet and the individual, and the goal is to make that link as strong as possible. The success of your poppet is dictated by how effectively you direct your intention. Your personalization of your poppet—the very act of creating it—directs that intention and forms a connection.

For example, you might sew or attach items to the poppet. These items could represent someone's desires, needs, or ailments as part of a spell. If you are performing a spell for someone to have more love in their life, you could attach a heart or a similar love talisman or symbol to the poppet. If you want someone to have good fortune, you could attach a talisman or symbol of good fortune as part of your spell, or even some money. If you are casting a spell to support someone's recovery, highlighting the area of ailment focuses your intent for their return to good health. Healing, spiritual renewal, protection, love spells, and even curses are possible, depending on your intent. Remember, your creativity and intent are the engine for your practice. Your poppet doesn't have to look perfect to work perfectly. In building your poppet, you've created a symbolic link to the person benefiting from your spell.

The personalization step can get very elaborate. It can involve color magick, gems, herbs, flowers, spices, and dirt, as well as taglocking. Taglocking is a powerful step in magick, employing the use of drawing symbols or sigils on the poppet and using personal items of the individual benefiting from your spellwork. I will share more information about these aspects in later chapters.

The final step is charging or enspiriting your poppet—in other words, making it work. After that, practitioners may perform actions on the poppet with the intention of influencing the corresponding individual. For example, in a healing spell, the poppet is manipulated or treated in a manner that symbolically addresses the ailments or imbalances of the person it represents. Poppets can be used for protection, emotional or otherwise, with actions performed on the doll intended to ward off negative energies or prevent harm from reaching the person. Poppets can also be used to symbolically cut ties, helping people move on from past relationships and let go of tethers to unhealthy situations. Again, poppet magick is all about your intent.

The Art Part

I want to return to the "art" in "arts and crafts," which my students often refer to as the "art part." This causes many people anxiety when learning about poppet magick. As shared in the beginning of this section, there is no artistic skill required for the creation of a poppet. That said, the more you develop your own style, the more you create your own signature in your craft. This will add to your manifestation, so be fearless. Make it your own.

Again, you can make your poppet out of almost any material, and *material* is a word with a broad definition. I like working with fabric. It's versatile, forgiving, and comes in a wide range of colors and textures. So, for the sake of example, let's talk poppet creation using fabric.[12] Classic felt can be inexpensively purchased in lots of colors. Using an old T-shirt that is yours (or that belonged to the person you are making the poppet for) will help with personalization and taglocking. I advise using biodegradable and natural cloth whenever possible, especially if it is eventually going to be buried or burned. The same goes for materials; with all ingredients and additives, try to use everything as organically as you can. Stay away from plastics and too many synthetic ingredients. They are not environmentally sound, and natural ingredients tend to conduct magick better anyway.

---

12. If you are interested in other media, such as dough or string, you can find more about those in part III of this book.

From the very beginning, make sure you are focused and putting your intent into everything you do. Remember your intention even during early steps such as gathering, shopping, cutting, stuffing, or sewing. That is a huge secret to success for your poppet and your spell. The entire process is part of the spellwork, even driving to a craft store or shopping online. The more you put into it, the more you will get out of it!

Choosing Other Ingredients

I must reiterate again that you can make a poppet out of practically anything. Pick a medium that speaks to you and that will not distract you from focusing on your intent. It would be a shame if the method you chose was so difficult that it drew your focus away from why you're creating the poppet in the first place! For example, if you have never tried a potter's wheel before but you're great with Play-Doh, then stick to what you know. The poppet will be more effective in the long run.

Once you have decided on the medium you will be using to create your poppet, return to your intent. Visualize the energy and attributes you need to achieve your goal. You want a calm, clear resolution, so take the time to research what colors, herbs, materials, crystals, symbols, or sigils can aid you in this quest; I'll explore quite a few in upcoming chapters. This is true whether you are making a poppet from scratch or are planning to purchase and personalize one. Ask yourself what objects or crafting you'll need to personalize the poppet, then add taglocks, such as hair or nails, to focus your intention.

Buying a Poppet

If doing any kind of art is a sticking point, do not let that stop you from poppet magick. Consider buying a poppet form. Some practitioners would rather focus on the design and spellwork than the creation of the poppet itself. For those who do, there are beautiful premade poppets you can buy that can then be personalized. I have seen premade poppets that feature tiny zippers where you can stuff your own ingredients and others that have little pockets for personal items.

Craft stores sometimes have very reasonably priced muslin dolls available to purchase. These are ready-made dolls that have stuffing in them. A muslin doll will give you a good base to work with for an affordable price; search online for "12 inch muslin doll" and see what you can find. If you do purchase a small muslin doll, I recommend cutting a little slice into it that you can use as a pocket. You could also sew, glue, or pin on a pocket. This way, you can personalize the poppet with desired herbs, items, and taglocks.

You can also use commercially available, store-bought dolls as poppets. I especially like store-bought dolls when I want to keep a magickal poppet in a public place without anyone knowing it is a poppet. For example, a superhero doll could be used as a protection poppet and placed in your child's bedroom on a shelf. Get creative. Everything from Barbies to princess dolls work great as poppets too; really, you can use any non-haunted doll that you already own.

Cleansing a Store-Bought Poppet

If you decide to purchase a store-bought doll for your poppet magick, or if you are going to use a doll you already own, cleanse it before starting your poppet creation. You can find instructions on cleansing your purchased poppet or non-haunted doll for use as a poppet in chapter 10.

To summarize, remove any packaging and sit with the doll. I like to first offer gratitude to everyone involved in the creation of the doll, including the people and/or machines that made the doll, those who packaged the doll, and those who drove it to the store where I bought it. Gratitude is always a good place to start.

Next, use smoke to cleanse the doll. I recommend palo santo. A light sprinkling of Florida water will also work beautifully. Remember, your intent is the most powerful ingredient in all your magick.

Once the poppet feels clear (trust your intuition), sit with the empty vessel for a few minutes before starting the process of creating the poppet.

Ethics in Magick

Before going further, I must touch on the subject of ethical poppet magick. Always respect the free will and well-being of others. I cannot emphasize this strongly enough: Ethical considerations should always be made when working with poppets or any other form of magickal practice. I already mentioned this in regard to love spells, but ethical consideration applies to all spellwork.

Remember, poppets can be used for positive and negative magick. I personally only use poppets for positive magick because I believe that you must live in the world you create, and I wouldn't want somebody to make a negative poppet of me. With that being said, poppets do work well when you need to bind somebody who is wishing you ill or doing you wrong. If that sounds like powerful magick, it can be. It can also be empowering, depending on the intent you put into your craft. Intent is everything.

Chapter 10

Magickal Considerations

If you are still interested in creating your own poppet, then you are in for a treat. They truly are super fun to make. If I can do it, anyone can—I have no artistic ability! However, I have found that enthusiasm and channeling my energy make up for my lack of artistic finesse.

Again, I cannot emphasize enough that your main ingredient is your intention. Your artistic ability is not a factor in your poppet's success. With any other kind of spellwork and magick, you must focus your thoughts through action—in this case, through the creation of this object and your interactions with it.

Poppet Materials and Ingredients

Be mindful when choosing your poppet material and the ingredients for your poppet. These supplies all symbolically contribute to your goal. Whether your intention is money, love, healing, binding, protection, or something else, begin by making a list of potential ingredients, including herbs, crystals, fabric, yarn, written words, sigils, etc. Then, cross out any ingredients that do not direct more power to your intent.

Think of your poppet as a story. By carefully choosing your poppet's ingredients, you are building the narrative for your spell. Getting to know the history and culture of your ingredients also deepens understanding and your connection to the thousands of magickal practitioners who have made and used poppets just as you are right now.

Want to blaze your own trail? There's no harm in being original. You can get creative with your poppet additives! You could put photos, drawings, or charms inside of them. You can include anything you have made to really tie the poppet to yourself or another person, whether or not the ingredient is considered "traditional."

While we are on the topic of nontraditional ingredients, remember that energy is also a powerful ingredient! In fact, energy is my favorite invisible ingredient. If you do Reiki or other healing modalities, you can add them to the poppet. Charge the poppet with energy by putting your hands around the doll and saying, "I am charging this poppet to this magickal energy and practice." It's fun, easy, and empowering. Read the full instructions for your poppet's charging in chapter 15.

Cleansing Your Ingredients

After choosing your ingredients, you should cleanse them. If you have purchased a premade poppet, you should cleanse it as well, along with anything else you have purchased or brought in including string, herbs, stones, and other personalization items. To be clear, cleansing doesn't mean busting out dishwashing soap and a scrub brush—it means a spiritual cleanse. A spiritual cleanse ensures that all your ingredients are free from negative energies, whether they carried a negative spiritual energy or the energy from a store clerk having a bad day. The goal here is to neutralize the energy of your ingredients before you create and activate your poppet.

Cleansing can be done in several ways, ranging from simple to complex. Let's start with some of the easiest. Leave your ingredients in direct sunlight for a few hours, or leave your ingredients under direct moonlight overnight. It's as simple as that! No extra equipment needed, and no assembly required. With that said, you should be aware of effects the sun might have on your items before leaving them in the sunlight. Wax figures, for example, may not survive the sun if exposed to high temperatures. Alternatively, some ingredients may not be waterproof. So, watch the weather.

If you have an herb you can burn, you can cleanse your ingredients with smoke. Consider burning palo santo, cedar, or juniper, either as a dried herb or as an incense.

Another easy way to cleanse your ingredients is to use a selenite stone. Selenite is a type of crystallized gypsum that naturally cleanses the items around it. If you have a piece of selenite, leave your ingredients by the stone for a night.

You can also devise more complex ways of cleansing your ingredients if that feels more natural to you. Your cleansing process may even become part of your signature style! For example, you could bury your poppet ingredients in your garden overnight, under the light of a full moon. Just remember where you buried them so you can find them the next day.

Sacred Space

Creating your poppet is just like cooking, baking, crafting, working out, and anything else you take seriously: You will need a dedicated space, even if it's temporary. This is an essential tool in poppet work. You should establish sacred space regardless of the materials you are using to build or personalize your poppet.

To create a sacred space for poppet making, there are five essential components:

1. A space with minimal distractions
2. All your poppet ingredients and crafting tools
3. The mood

4. Your deities or guides, if applicable
5. The plan

It's essential that your sacred space is free from distractions, clutter, and possible interruptions. Your focus should not be disrupted by your favorite show, your phone, or your familiar jumping on your work surface every five minutes. One hundred percent of your focus should be on the task at hand: creating a successful poppet.

In the previous section, I shared how to cleanse your ingredients before use. After they have been cleansed, you can place all of your ingredients and tools in your sacred space. Organize the ingredients and tools in a way that feels right for you, ensuring you can see all of the items to focus your intent. Visualize what you're about to do.

Next, set the mood. Perhaps light candles or dim the lights. You could light some incense; sandalwood is my favorite, but use what you like. You can also play soft or inspiring music if it helps you set the tone for the work.

You're now in a space to work within your path to call in spirits or deities, call corners, or cast a circle. There is no right or wrong way to do this; just do what you need to so that the space becomes sacred to you.

The last essential component is a plan for your spellwork. Can you diverge from that plan? Of course! Go wherever the spirit(s) moves you as you create. Just start from a place that will allow you to focus and complete your intended poppet.

Intention Is Everything

As you will begin to see over the next few chapters, there is a whole universe of ingredients for poppet stuffing out there. However, the main ingredient in the creation of your poppet is—you guessed it—intent. That intention, and the focus you use to pour it into the creation of your poppet, gives a poppet its power. In other words, intent is what differentiates poppet creation from arts and crafts.

I have used poppets for protection, courage, confidence, love, luck, binding, and even inner child and shadow work. Poppets provide a great visual, are terrific for focusing your intentions, and are especially great to use in spiritual practice for getting rid of bad habits, destructive behaviors, and even toxic relationships.

Now, let's make some poppets.

CHAPTER 11

Color Magick

I like paying attention to colors and their magickal correspondences when creating poppets. Color magick is an important and potent part of spellcrafting. Color magick can be represented by the materials/medium used, thread, gems, drawn-on symbols or words, different colors of paint, ink, powder, glitter, or food coloring, to name a few options.

For example, red thread is often used in the creation of poppets. Red is a color associated with energy, passion, and strength. It is often linked to matters of the heart, love, and relationships. Red can symbolize courage and protection. Therefore, by incorporating red thread, you can imbue the poppet with these qualities or intentions. Red is also the color of blood, which is associated with life force and vitality. So, the color red can help you tap into the vital essence of the person the poppet represents.

While red is a popular choice, I don't believe there are any hard and fast "rules" to poppet creation, so I often use another thread color if it has an attribute or correspondence I want to add to my poppet. You can also use more than one color of thread. Your poppet can be as colorful as you'd like.

I've listed some color correspondences here for general reference. These are generally accepted but not set in stone. I always advocate for going with what feels right to you, no matter what anyone else says!

White

It might be surprising to learn that white is actually a very complicated color with multiple, sometimes seemingly contradictory, meanings. It's actually the combination of every color, yet it has its own specific set of properties and meanings.

White is the color of purity, cleansing, spiritual connection, healing, and protection. It's both the color of birth and of death, depending on the culture. The meanings are similar when you think of white as a color of purity and passage; at birth and death, we are in our purest states. Both events underline our spiritual connection to the universe. The states of purity and passage of the color white have been symbolized in bridal dresses for more than a century. This is a strange turn of events because not long ago, it was common for mourners to wear white. In some traditions, like Sikhism, white is still the color of mourning. It's unknown how long the color white has been used to represent spiritual connection, but Paleolithic cave dwellers used chalk and limestone powders at least as far back as 40,000 BCE.

And then there are white foods, all of which have their own connotations. White foods like salt, table sugar, and milk have magickal healing properties, both by themselves and when used together. In its purest form, salt is white, and it is often used for protection.

In addition to its spiritual connection and protective properties, white is also the color of healing. In ancient Greece, those attending the Asclepieion, a renowned place of healing, wore white for treatment at the Temple of Hygeia (where we get the word *hygiene*).[13]

In other words, however you are using the color white, it is powerful.

White Ingredients for Poppet Work

- String, candles, buttons, fabric, or paint
- Moonstone, clear quartz, or other white stones and crystals

Pink

Feeling "in the pink" is a real thing. Historically, this phrase meant good health, but it has come to mean "optimal." In Renaissance times, pink was

13. Ferris, "Connecting the Mind and Body in Ancient Greek Medicine."

considered the color of perfection. It still represents both things. That's because pink is the color of inner contentment, acceptance, and the experience of joy in connection with others. Pink is the color of affection. It's friendship, healing, emotional well-being, love, and self-love.

Pink is an incredibly positive color. Picture a pink glow—whether it's a pale pink, neon pink, bubblegum, or magenta—radiating outward from your heart space and connecting with your partner, your family, your friends, your community, and the world. How does that make you feel? It makes me feel "in the pink."

Pink Ingredients for Poppet Work

- String, candles, buttons, fabric, or paint
- Dried pink flowers, like pink roses, which are a high-vibration flower
- Pink stones such as rose quartz (my go-to, especially for love poppets) or pink tourmaline

Red

The color red really is the color of the heart, and I love working with it. I associate it with passion, sensual love, courage, strength, vitality, energy, and power. There are other powerful colors, but I see red as "firepower."

Fire red fuels the power of courage and the strength and drive to complete monumental tasks. It's the vitality that keeps you going.

There is also the deep, sensual red of passion, no matter what that passion happens to be. Of course, it's also the color of corporeal love, from a burning ember to an engulfing *amour fou*.

Red Ingredients for Poppet Work

- String, candles, buttons, fabric, or paint
- Flowers like roses, poppies, daylilies, tulips, or chrysanthemums
- Red stones like garnet, ruby, or coral (my favorite "heart" stone; I often use a piece of coral in my poppets in the heart space)
- A red heart sewn or drawn on the poppet

Orange

No other color matches the exuberance of orange. It's always attention-grabbing and energizing. Therefore, if you feel blocked or if your head is not in the game, consider going for orange.

Use orange to boost your creativity, enthusiasm, attraction, success, joy, and energy. It's the look-at-me color, so it's the color of successful engagement. Bright orange radiates joy and attracts positive attention. Rich orange invites creativity. Does it make you hungry? It should—creativity is food for the soul. Light orange and peach have a delicious connection to the sensual world, hence the color's association with attraction.

Orange Ingredients for Poppet Work

- String, candles, buttons, fabric, or paint
- Dried orange peel
- Flowers like orange marigolds, roses, chrysanthemums, or tiger lilies
- Orange stones like fire opals or carnelian (for courage)

Yellow

Want a magickal pick-me-up? Go for the gold. The color yellow signifies success, confidence, clarity, intellectual pursuits, and communication. Yellow is the unofficial color of the "Aha!" moment, where you are able to see the problem *and* a clear understanding of the solution. There are shades like lemon yellow, buttery yellow, bright sunflower yellow, rich gold, and warming ochre. When you use the color yellow, you are harnessing sunlight. And, as the saying goes, sunlight is the best disinfectant.

Use your sunshine-yellow power to open lines of communication. Use lemon yellow to cleanse and clear your perspective. Incorporate sunflower yellow and harvest gold to reap success. Use rich gold as a halo to invite in a divine spark of knowledge. Feel the inner confidence of natural ochre—a pigment used since the Stone Age—as it warms you from the inside out.

Yellow Ingredients for Poppet Work

- String, candles, buttons, fabric, or paint
- Dried yellow flowers, like marigolds, hibiscus, roses, or mums
- Stones like citrine or topaz

Green

There is a literal wealth of meaning in the color green. Its renewing energy calls to mind prosperity, abundance, growth, fertility, luck, and healing. The color green's spectrum of natural shades wraps you in good fortune, from the deep green of juniper and pine to the prosperous brilliance of emerald. Intense, vibrant greens evoke personal growth and fertility, while spring greens remind us of regeneration, renewal, and healing. What's the luckiest shade of green? Why, it's your favorite, of course!

Green Ingredients for Poppet Work

- String, candles, buttons, fabric, or paint
- Dried flowers like zinnias, orchids, or even green roses
- Stones like jade, malachite, or green aventurine (I use this in wealth poppets)

Blue

Whether you're standing on the beach, staring at the sea, or relaxing on a hillside and staring at the clear blue sky, nothing beats the calming, meditative focus of blue. It's no wonder that it's the color of peace, calm, universal communication, emotional healing, and emotional intuition. It's easy to see the clouds in someone else's gaze when your own perspective is clear and centered, so ease into the calm energy that is sky blue. Bring about emotional healing with the deep, intense colors of the sea. Find revelatory emotional connection with brilliant sapphire blues.

Blue Ingredients for Poppet Work

- String, candles, buttons, fabric, or paint
- Dried flowers like morning glories, cornflowers, or petunias
- Stones like lapis lazuli, larimar, sapphire, iolite, blue quartz, blue agate, turquoise, or labradorite (my current favorite for emotional healing)

Purple

It's difficult to think of a time in which the color purple was not the color of royalty and the spiritual realm. At least as far back as 1600 BCE, people from Tyre were taking extractions from *Murex* mollusks to create the first purple dye. These ancient Phoenicians became so famous for their purple dye that the shade became known as "Tyrian purple."[14] Because it was difficult to acquire, purple dye was ultra expensive, reserved for priests, monarchs, and the wealthy.

The color purple has always evoked spirituality, psychic abilities, intuition, wisdom, and transformation. Intensely vibrant purples, violets, plums, and even lavender colors impact our connection to higher powers and to the spiritual world, as well as to our own intuition. Shades of purple connect to the psychic abilities in all of us and invite spiritual transformation due to their energetic high vibration.

Purple Ingredients for Poppet Work

- String, candles, buttons, fabric, or paint
- Dried lavender, salvia, violet, petunias, mums, or other purple flowers
- Stones like amethyst (my all-time favorite stone for connecting to the spirit world), tanzanite, alexandrite, purple agate, or purple quartz

Black

If you have ever mixed together every color of paint on a palette, you know that black is the sum of all colors when mixed. However, the color black

14. Podhajny, "History, Shellfish, Royalty, and the Color Purple."

is technically the complete absence of color. Black is my absolute favorite color to work with. This duality of the complete attraction of color and the rejection of it makes black the ideal color for protection, banishing negativity, absorbing positive energy, and dispelling negative energy. I like to use the color black when working with protective symbols, including the Helm of Awe. I often use black thread on my poppets to absorb positive energy and let go of negativity.

Black Ingredients for Poppet Work

- String, candles, buttons, fabric, or paint
- Dried flowers including black dahlias, black calla lilies, black petunias, black day lilies, or black tulips
- Stones like black tourmaline (often used in healing poppets because of its remarkable healing powers), jet, or onyx

Brown

Using brown, earthy tones in your practice allows you a variety of possibilities. Brown not only represents grounding, stability, practicality, home life, and family matters, it makes a terrific modifier or "helper" color. Need to jumpstart passion in your home life? Look no further than mineral-based brown/red colors like sienna, cherrywood, and red ochre. Want to focus on your psychic abilities while remaining on stable ground? Try purple-brown colors like chocolate.

Brown Ingredients for Poppet Work

- String, candles, buttons, fabric, or paint
- Dirt
- Petrified wood
- Non-perishable cocoa products like cocoa mulch (smells like chocolate!)
- Brown flowers like brown or beige roses, chocolate-colored petunias, day lilies, or brown orchids
- Stones like tiger's eye, brown agate, topaz, or smoky quartz

Color is a wonderful addition to your poppet magick. Just like with other ingredients, when you work with color, your truth or feeling about what that color represents is more important than what a book, a chart, or anybody else says.

CHAPTER 12

Herbs, Spices, and Flowers

Two wonderful things about using herbs, spices, and flowers as ingredients are their versatility and their engagement of the senses. As a sensual ingredient, you can see their beauty and experience them through touch, smell, and (sometimes) taste. You can use herbs, spices, and flowers in fresh, dried, crushed, or powdered forms; they are also often found in essential oil form. Need eucalyptus for a healing spell? You don't necessarily need a whole sprig when you can just add a drop or two of essential oil.

I always stuff my poppets with the herbs and flowers that most align with my intention. In this chapter, you'll find some fun facts about the herbs and flowers I use most often. As I mentioned in chapter 10, the point of reviewing the historical and cultural uses of ingredients is to create building blocks for the story behind your poppet's spell. If any of these ingredients speak to you, use them as you build the story of your own poppet, and your spell will be that much more effective. The more thought you put into the creation story of your poppet, and the more considered your approach, the more focused and powerful your intent will be.

In this list, you'll find ingredients from the ancient to the everyday. I have listed them according to specific purpose so you can refer back to this chapter whenever you are planning poppet magick.

For Money

My favorite herbs and flowers for use in money poppets are extremely versatile. It's wonderful when you can find them fresh, which can be possible depending on what part of the world you live in. But it's relatively easy to get these ingredients as essential oils, and often you'll even be able to find them in dried form. If you're like me, the first place you might want to look is your kitchen cupboard. Somewhere in the back of your pantry may be a sachet containing chamomile tea, or perhaps some cinnamon tea you bought when you had a cold. Any form of the ingredient will do as long as it isn't already mixed in with something else. For example, pesto sauce, though delicious, does not count as basil.

Basil

Basil is known for attracting abundance and prosperity. Give me this green any day! According to the Oxford English Dictionary, the word *basil* is derived from the ancient Greek *basileus*, meaning "king," so it's a natural choice for anyone looking to put some prosperity in their poppet.[15] It's funny to think that basil was so feared by Northern Europeans that they avoided it like, well, you know. In the book *The English Physitian*, written in 1652, Nicholas Culpeper says of basil, "Hilarius, a French playwright, affirms upon his own knowledge, that an acquaintance of his, by common smelling to it, had a scorpion bred in his brain."[16] It's unknown whether or not Culpeper ever saw a basil plant in person, but scorpion growth has not been reported since.

What is true of basil is that it is a beautiful herb, full of robust flavor and a wonderful scent. Basil has broad, glossy leaves that are sometimes an intense green, sometimes bright purple, depending on the variety. White or purple flowers emerge in spires above the leaves. Basil can be relatively easy to grow into a happy, productive plant for those who care for it. Keeping a tidy, well-fed plant also means an abundance of edible leaves on a plant that lasts. That may be another reason why wealth and prosperity are

15. Dean, "The Etymology of Basil."

16. Calder, "Plant 327."

associated with basil. Perhaps the message of basil is "Tend to your wealth, and abundance will flow." After all, some gamblers put a basil leaf in their pocket before hitting the casino.

Chamomile

Chamomile is often used to attract money and bring good fortune in financial matters. Calming, soothing chamomile has a double life as a money attractant and a good luck talisman. The word *chamomile* refers to a group of slender plants with happy, daisy-like flowers. This plant is used all over the world, and it has been since ancient times. As you can see by walking down grocery store aisles, chamomile is still used as a medicine and a tea, and it is even used in the kitchen.

Chamomile has a fascinating history. It is mentioned in many early medical texts—including the Ebers papyrus, circa 1550 BCE—for its calming and soothing properties. Wealthy Egyptians used chamomile in cosmetics. It was also a regular offering to the sun god Ra, thought to be a divine gift. Chamomile oil sometimes anointed the bodies of pharaohs during Egyptian funerary practices. It is also one of the nine sacred herbs listed in the *Lacnunga*, an Anglo-Saxon compilation of remedies from the tenth century.

The tradition of gamblers washing their hands with chamomile water/tea dates back at least hundreds of years. Maybe that's why chamomile is thought to bring good fortune. Perhaps the sun will shine upon those who use this modest and helpful herb.

Cinnamon

Associated with success and financial growth, cinnamon has a wealth of flavor. It's also one of the oldest spices to be traded and is native to Sri Lanka. Ancient Egypt was crazy for cinnamon and used it in the embalming process as well as in medicines, perfumes, and cooking. Cinnamon was hard to get and expensive, so it was a status symbol for those who could afford it. By medieval times, it was used in seven spice (cinnamon, cloves, cumin, coriander, pepper, ginger, and cardamon or nutmeg) and *baharat* (a sweet-hot mixture of rosebuds and cinnamon) in and around Persia. Imagine the heavenly smell of that sweet-hot mixture!

Cassia is extremely similar to cinnamon and is related botanically, though it comes from a different plant. Cassia is also known as "Chinese cinnamon." If you're a fan of Cinnabon, that cinnamon is Indonesian Korintje cinnamon. Both Indonesian cinnamon and Chinese cinnamon have similar rich, bright, hot flavor and can be swapped with true cinnamon in your practice with no problems whatsoever. You may even prefer it!

With all its history, it's easy to see how the richness of flavor and the wealth associated with cinnamon make it a perfect match for financial success.

Patchouli

Patchouli is believed to bring financial luck and increase business opportunities. Taking a look at its history will illustrate why patchouli is a fantastic "business prosperity" herb.

Patchouli grows wild in Java and Sumatra at heights between 3,000 and 6,000 feet. It's an unassuming, bushy, broad-leafed plant with pink flowers, and it grows up to three feet tall. It's thought that this perennial herb was first used by the Tamil people (who referred to it as *pacchilai*) as an insect repellent and as a medicinal tea. Its use spread, and patchouli's strong scent gave a pleasant odor to fabrics, repelled moths, and covered body odor, among other uses. Then this herb really hit its stride. Using patchouli in trade in South Asia and the Middle East for scenting high ticket textiles and, really, for pest control became prevalent. By the 1840s, the British and other Europeans became massive fans of patchouli and its strong, pleasing, and moth-repelling smell. Europeans couldn't get enough of the rich fragrance used on their imported, richly colored, fine fabrics, and subsequently patchouli became an in-demand essential oil in Western culture. This is likely where its association with wealth in business comes from.

Of course, none of that information detracts from the fact that many people do not care for the smell of patchouli at all. That might be because some people have the habit of substituting patchouli for modern deodorant.... Turns out the two are not interchangeable.

For Love

There are so many good herbs, spices, and flowers for love magick. Some of the items you could put in your love poppet are orange peel, cardamom, dill, lemon, red clover, ash, hibiscus, bay, rosemary, coriander, angelica, burdock, dragon's blood, fern, ginger, and hawthorn. Here are a few of my all-time favorites.

Damiana

Damiana is associated with love spells and enhancing passion. I love using this flower in poppets because of its unusual properties. A word of warning: There can be serious side effects if damiana is ingested, including severe, life-threatening reactions. But since you're stuffing it in your poppet, you shouldn't have to worry about that.

For generations, damiana has been used in traditional medicine as everything from an aphrodisiac to a cure for venereal disease. You can find damiana growing naturally from the southern tip of Texas down to South America and everywhere in between. It has happy, cute yellow flowers that bely its passionate reputation. It's a perfect addition for anyone wanting to add a little lust to their love spell.

Jasmine

This flower is often used to attract love and enhance sensuality. There are several kinds of jasmine, and any will work for your practice. Don't worry about which is the "proper" version of the plant; use what you have access to. After all, it is your intent that matters.

There are over two hundred wonderfully scented varieties of jasmine, but the jasmine we most associate with the smell of teas and perfumes is Arabian jasmine. It's also known as sambac jasmine. It's native to South Asia, and farmers there harvested it for trade. Jasmine made its way across the ancient world, and it popped up in Egypt. The Egyptians fell head over heels in love with jasmine's smell. It was very popular, and they celebrated it in Egyptian art, design, and writing.

Imagine traders from China and South Asia and Persia smelling jasmine for the first time. It can lull you into a sensuous trance. That's why I use it.

Lavender

Lavender promotes love, harmony, and emotional well-being. Pure, balanced love, the kind of love you find at the end of an English costume drama.

Lavender is a type of mint with more than thirty varieties found in countries around the Mediterranean. Any one of several lavenders (English, French, Spanish, Arabian, etc.) will do in your poppet. I have a few varieties of lavender growing in my garden, and I have no idea where they come from. "English lavender," one of the most popular types, came to Britain with the Romans. Its name comes from the Latin *lavare* ("to wash"), and this spectacular purple flower with its gray-green leaves was indeed used to scent Roman baths.

Lavender is a handy herb with a lovely flavoring. It's also been a scent of courtly love. In Henry VIII's England, lavender was used in everything from cushions to candle wax. Lavender was also used in washing, so much so that washerwomen were often called "lavenders." Queen Elizabeth I loved her lavender. It was all over the English court: It was viewed as hygienic, masked other odors, and was frequently used as a cure-all. What's not to love?

Rose Petals

Rose petals symbolize love and romance. There are few symbols of love more enduring than a rose. In Greek myth, the red rose is said to be the result of Aphrodite, the goddess of love, shedding tears that mixed with the blood of her slain lover, Adonis. Roses are synonymous with love and beauty, at least for William Shakespeare: "That which we call a rose / By any other word would smell as sweet."[17] In one of her origin stories, the Hindu goddess Lakshmi, wife of Vishnu, was created out of rose petals.

---

17. Shakespeare, *The Tragedy of Romeo and Juliet*, 2.2.46–47. References are to act, scene, and line.

Wild roses are everywhere. They grow in many places across the globe, from the Arctic to the southern tip of Asia. The fruits of the rose are called "rose hips." Rose hips are widely used in flavorings, teas, perfumes, and medicine. Today, there are even roses bred for these uses.

Mesopotamian cuneiform tablets indicate that roses became known to humans about 3000 BCE. Although we don't know exactly what rose the ancient world used for rosewater and decoration, they were fairly small, somewhat thornier, and delicate compared to today's massive and sturdy florist's blooms.

The best example is the damask rose, still in use today. A full damask rose has around forty petals and is heavily scented. Damask rose is that heady rose fragrance that stops you in your tracks. Damask rose farms throughout Eurasia now provide the world with the scent of romance. With that being said, the best roses for use in your practice are the ones you can find in your own backyard. Fun fact: If you have ever wondered how many rose petals are in one cup, the answer is about forty-five.

For Health

In this section, you'll find poppet stuffings that can help heal most ailments. These herbs, spices, and flowers are a great place to start, and I always have them on hand. However, as you develop your practice, you may want to branch out and include a few other healing herbs. I sometimes like to include angelica, dill, ginger, allspice, coltsfoot, coriander, burdock, self-heal, skullcap, or thyme in my healing spells, depending on whom I'm making the poppet for.

Calendula

Calendula is used in healing spells to enhance vitality. Calendula flowers are marigolds, but not all marigolds are calendula flowers. You know those crisp, multi-petalled, ruffled flowers that look like carnations with a splashy, attention-grabbing yellow, orange, or reddish-orange makeover? Those are not calendula. Calendula comes in the same attention-grabbing colors but, unlike what we think of as marigolds (technically the *Tagetes* genus or Mexican marigolds), they possess daisy-like flowers.

Calendula flowers are edible, raw or cooked, and they have been used as everything from a flavor-enhancer to a clothing dye for centuries. They were used widely in both Ayurvedic (ancient Indian) and Unani (ancient Greek) systems of medicine. This beautiful plant may be helpful in growing new tissue, healing wounds, and decreasing inflammation. Calendula may be harder to come by than the other kind of marigold, but you can get seeds or oils to add to your poppet online or at your nearest garden store. It's well worth it.

Eucalyptus

Eucalyptus is known for its healing properties and promoting overall well-being. There's nothing quite like inhaling the smell of eucalyptus when you're feeling low. It clears your sinuses and opens up your third eye. As an olfactory pick-me-up, this Australian wonder tree is great, but it is so much more than that.

You can stuff your poppet with any bit of the seven hundred or so types of eucalyptus, from the peeling bark of the giant gum trees to the little potted plants you can buy at a nursery. It all works. However, if you are looking for something, well, pungent, I would recommend bark or oils from the blue gum. You can pick that up under its Latin name, *Eucalyptus globulus*, or look for a eucalyptus tree in the park. Nature is effective!

I'd also recommend a couple of lesser-known varieties, depending on the needs of your intended healing spell. Try Forth River peppermint (*Eucalyptus radiata*) for a slightly sweeter kick; this is a great option in healing spells for a lung ailment. You may want to try the camphor-y blue peppermint eucalyptus (*Eucalyptus dives*) in a healing spell for muscle aches, or soothing lemon-scented eucalyptus (*Corymbia citriodora*) for a healing spell for laryngitis. Before you raid your local tree farm, know that all of these varieties are available as essential oils as well. Also, don't let the names fool you; eucalyptus trees do not contain peppermint.

Peppermint

Peppermint is associated with physical healing and boosting energy. It is mentioned in Egyptian medical texts dating back to 1550 BCE and is technically a hybrid of spearmint and watermint. However, peppermint is more intense in flavor and contains more menthol than regular mint.

Peppermint is such a great pick-me-up. It has an energizing smell and cool taste, and yet it can warm you as you rub it into your skin. Peppermint is used for stomach upset and IBS. Who doesn't like a nice cup of peppermint tea to aid digestion? So, if you're creating a poppet healing spell for skin ailments, muscle injuries, soreness, tightness, or stomach ailments such as aches or pains, look no further than peppermint.

Of course, that's not all this little herb represents. Use peppermint as the great energizer, to boost energy as well as healing. Make it part of your poppet's healing spell to promote healing of bodily aches and pains *and* to have the energy to get through the process as well! Incidentally, accept no substitutions.

Rosemary

Rosemary is believed to bring physical and mental health and protection from illness. There is a wonderful quote about rosemary that pretty much sums up why it is so useful for physical and mental well-being. Roger Hacket, a doctor of divinity who lived in the 1500s, said, "Speaking of the powers of rosemary, it overtoppeth all the flowers in the garden, boasting man's rule. It helpeth the brain, strengtheneth the memorie, and is very medicinable for the head. Another property of the rosemary is, it affects the heart."[18]

Students in ancient Greece wore wreaths of rosemary to improve their studying and learning abilities. Traditions going back millennia used sprigs of rosemary to encourage mourners to remember the deceased. In Shakespeare's *Hamlet*, teenage Ophelia gives medicinal herbs: "There's rosemary, that's for remembrance. / Pray you, love, remember."[19] This is one powerful herb!

Any form of rosemary will do for your poppet. It's available dried, with its spikey leaves removed from the stalks. It's also available fresh, as a garden plant, or you may see it in a public garden or park as a groundcover.

For Luck

By pure coincidence, three of the herbs and spices I like to use when stuffing a luck poppet happen to be some of the most popular smells found in the autumnal baked goods and mulled cider of Western tradition. No wonder everyone loves the smell of pumpkin spice lattes!

---

18. Grieve, *A Modern Herbal*.

19. Shakespeare, *Hamlet*, 4.5.199–200. References are to act, scene, and line.

Allspice

Allspice is associated with luck and abundance. It was used in Indigenous traditions long before the arrival of the Spaniards at Ay-ti (Hispaniola), and by the Arawak and the Mayans in their embalming practices and medicine. It was also used as a flavoring for everything from drinking chocolate to meat preservation.

Dried allspice can be found whole or powdered in the spice aisle of your local market. Allspice is sometimes burned to attract luck and abundance. Remember, you don't have to burn anything for poppet magick; the addition of allspice is enough.

Cloves

There is a long-standing tradition of using cloves to attract luck and prosperity. This association reportedly comes from the Hindu festival of Navratri, which is a biannual celebration that honors the goddess Durga. Devotees wishing for Durga to grant them luck can make an offering to her each day for the nine days of the festival. She is said to favor cloves and roses.[20]

Cloves are indigenous to Indonesia but were traded from the Eastern part of the Roman Empire in Damascus to China. The spice trade in the fourth century brought cloves to Europe. Cloves' ability to enhance good

20. "Want to Seek Goddess Durga's Blessings?"

flavors and mask bad ones made it a go-to for food preservation. Like a fad cure-all, cloves went viral. Europeans claimed that cloves improved dental health, cured inflammation, and gave you a better libido. When it became in demand as a high-ticket item, both Ferdinand Magellan and Frances Drake set out to find easier trade routes for the spice. Quite a history for these dried flower buds!

You can find dried whole or powdered cloves at your local supermarket. I like to use cloves in poppet luck spells as a magnet for good fortune.

Irish Moss

Irish moss is believed to bring good luck and protection. Irish moss is not exclusively Irish, not green, and not an actual moss. It is a type of seaweed grown in intertidal rocks. That means it's sometimes above water and sometimes below, but it's always there protecting the shore. You can find Irish moss on shorelines of the Atlantic coast, including in North America, the British Isles, and Europe.

Though Irish moss is harvested as a curly, rock-clinging seaweed, it's touted as a modern superfood and has been used as a food stuff by Europeans since at least the fifth century. The name "Irish moss" comes from the Irish potato famine of the nineteenth century. During the famine, as starving families were driven from place to place, the seaweed was a source of food and became their salvation. That's luck when you really need it.

Irish moss is available as a health food, and you can find it online in dried whole, powdered, or even gel form.

Nutmeg

Nutmeg is often used for luck, success, and increasing opportunities. I've been told that a whole nutmeg seed is needed to attract luck; I suppose that its egg shape has something to do with it. So, if you can get your hands on a whole nutmeg, then this poppet stuffing is for you.

Nutmeg is not a nut at all, but the seed inside the fruit of the *Myristica fragrans* tree. Incidentally, the spice known as mace is the dried lacy membrane that covers the seed's outer hull. Much of the noise around nutmeg—and there has been a lot—is from its former reputation as a "male enhancement." Whole nutmegs were once so expensive that suppliers would try and fake out customers with wooden duplicates!

Nutmeg comes from the Maluku Islands, a group of tiny islands between Indonesia and Papua New Guinea. They're just north of Timor and Northern Australia. It's a small amount of land for what became the most sought-after foodstuff on the planet in the 1500s and 1600s.

You can find powdered nutmeg fairly easily in the spice aisle. Some markets also sell whole nutmeg seeds, which are preferable if you can find them.

For Protection

The herbs I like to use for protection poppets have been around for eons. In my experience, it used to be hard to find these ancient remedies outside specialty stores, but they seem to be becoming more popular in recent years.

Black Salt

Black salt is not an herb, but a mixture of salt and protective herbs. There are many types of black salt. Black salt may refer to a type of dark pink sea salt; blended, flavored salts that happen to be dark in color; or *kala namak*, the most common type of black salt worldwide. Kala namak is kiln-fired salt from South Asia. In Northern India, it's traditionally roasted for about twenty-four hours, put in sealed ceramic containers with charcoal, and flavored with a blend of seeds and bark from local trees or natron.

In Ayurvedic medicine, black salt has been used in the treatment of everything from constipation to "hysteria."[21] Modern witches use black salt to create boundaries, to keep out evil spirits, and to create a safe space. Many versions of black salt can now be found online. Whatever version of black salt you get your hands on, you can use it on its own or as stuffing for your poppet. Place the black salt inside a small pouch alongside other herbs for added protection.

---

21. Jayaraman, "Health Benefit Uses of Black Salt."

Mugwort

Mugwort is associated with psychic protection and warding off negativity. Mugwort was a staple of Roman and medieval medicinal herb gardens. Roman soldiers put it in their footwear to prevent tired feet on long marches, amongst other uses. Medieval Europeans used mugwort to guard against fatigue while traveling, as protection against evil spirits and wild animals, and as an insect repellent. It was planted next to herbs with tender leaves to ward away garden pests.

After Europeans brought the plant to America, Indigenous peoples on the Atlantic Coast began using mugwort as a medicinal and spiritual aid. For example, rubbing one's body with mugwort was thought to keep ghosts away during the night.[22] This kind of mugwort should not be confused with Japanese mugwort, Chinese mugwort, or Korean mugwort, which are also highly useful herbs; I am talking about the common mugwort, now considered an invasive species in many places in the United States.

Mugwort may have escaped the confines of the garden, but it will be your protection if you find it before entering a dark forest or alongside a road in the middle of nowhere. When you find it, remember to gather a

22. Beall, "Mugwort."

little to stuff in your poppet. You can also grow your own mugwort or find it for sale dried, chopped, or powdered.

St. John's Wort

St. John's wort is often used to protect against negative influences and promote positivity. I love using St. John's wort because of its magickal connections to Hecate and Midsummer. In Greek tradition, it's said that Hecate, the goddess of magick, collected St. John's wort, and this yellow-flowered herb was used as an ingredient in spellcasting as a defense against evil. The Greeks called it *hyperikon*. In Northern Europe, St. John's wort was traditionally gathered on Midsummer Eve to ward off demons and despair. When the Catholic religion co-opted Pagan and non-Christian holidays to create their saints' "holy days," Midsummer became the feast day of John the Baptist; consequently, the little yellow flowers became known as St. John's wort.

There are many ways to use St. John's wort. You could carry some in your pocket, make a poppet with it and hang the poppet in your kitchen to safeguard against negative spells, or use the plant in teas and sachets to ward off depression and emotional ailments. St. John's wort can be grown if you have a green thumb and space in your garden. You can also find it sold dried, chopped, or even powdered.

Expanding Your Options

There are many excellent books about using natural ingredients in your practice. There are whole chapters written specifically about protection, a subject I've only touched upon here. For example, other herbs, spices, and flowers I often use for protection are rue, cedar, lavender, juniper, basil, burdock, blessed thistle, fern, mullein, lemon, devil's shoestring, angelica, anise, frankincense, wormwood, hyssop, thyme, and myrrh. For heavier protection, I might add black pepper, the poisonous belladonna, red pepper, tobacco, bone, cemetery dirt, or vinegar. I share this with you in the hopes that it will inspire you to do more research about the variety of herbs, spices, and flowers that are available.

Choose herbs, spices, and flowers that resonate with you and your specific intentions. Make sure that they are within your reach, whether that means you grow them yourself, find them at the grocery store, or stumble upon them in a friend's yard. You should be able to get your ingredients legally and safely without breaking the bank. Use your common sense. Always ensure that you are using herbs, spices, and flowers that are safe for such purposes, and take necessary precautions if you have allergies or sensitivities.

Chapter 13

Crystals, Stones, and Dirt

Crystals, stones, and dirt are powerful poppet ingredients. Sometimes I add a stone to represent my poppet's heart or to bring in the energy associated with the crystal. I may add dirt to bring in the vibrations from the place it was gathered from. In this chapter, I list some commonly used crystals and their attributes so they can be incorporated into your poppets. Then, I will share how to gather and use dirt, specifically graveyard dirt.

Stones and Crystals

When choosing crystals and stones for use in poppets, consider their energetic properties and correspondences, as you would with other ingredients. And remember, you don't have to break the bank. Finding gems is easier than you might think; just go to any well-stocked bead store or metaphysical shop.

Amethyst

Amethyst is a superb protection stone and a great choice for releasing bad habits. It's excellent for letting go of negative patterns, encouraging spiritual growth, and promoting self-care. Amethyst is a peaceful gem, a stone for dreamers. This stone deepens intuition; it opens the crown chakra and the third eye, granting clarity and foresight. Colors of amethyst range from pale lilac to dark grape. Other colors include pink, violet blue, or even wine red. Stones that have a banded *V* shape are called chevron amethyst. Chevron amethyst is particularly valued for its ability to enhance perception.

Keywords

- Spiritual growth
- Intuition
- Calm
- Protection

Black Tourmaline

Black stones deflect negative energy. Black tourmaline is terrific because, unlike other black stones, it deflects negative energy *and* attracts positive energy. That is why it's my favorite type of black stone! Paranormal investigators often wear black tourmaline for protection. This crystal grounds you in the earthly realm and disperses harmful energies—think of it as spiritual armor. It also aligns energy centers, making it an excellent healing stone and a terrific meditation stone. Black tourmaline aids in spiritual clarity, allowing you to see the path forward.

Keywords

- Protection
- Grounding
- Healing

Carnelian

Carnelian is a wonderful quartz with colors ranging from fire red to bright orange. If you're looking to boost motivation, passion, or mental clarity, carnelian is the perfect crystal. Its energetic warmth stimulates the drive to succeed while enhancing optimism. Carnelian can be used to decrease feelings of inadequacy and increase creative drive. It's also a stabilizing stone, used for emotional balance. Use carnelian in your poppet to empower the target of your spell and to motivate them to take consistent action.

Keywords

- Motivation
- Creativity
- Vitality
- Passion

Citrine

There is nothing like sunshine to brighten your day, and citrine has the ability to do just that. Citrine is a crystal that is most often clear, sunny yellow, but some stones include colors ranging from fireball red to sienna to near chartreuse. It's a money stone, an optimist's stone, a luck stone, a stone for abundance and financial success. I use citrine in poppet spells for luck, especially if the spell has to do with negotiating a raise. It's also a wonderful stone for self-confidence. Citrine removes self-destructive urges and silences that nagging voice of self-doubt. It gives you a can-do attitude. With citrine's help, you can manifest positivity. And who doesn't need a little more positivity in their life?

Keywords

- Abundance
- Manifestation
- Joy
- Self-confidence

Clear Quartz

If you are looking for balance and harmony, clear quartz is the stone for you. This stone can be used in any spell to amplify your intentions. It's a cleansing stone, so clear quartz can be used to heal and wash away ailments and negativity. Clear quartz can help encourage someone who is injured (whether it's a physical injury or an emotional injury) to begin healing. Additionally, this crystal is amazing for focus and clarity. You could use clear quartz in a poppet spell to heal a head cold, or use it on a day where mental acuity and focus are needed.

Keywords

- Amplification
- Clarity
- Healing
- Protection

Green Aventurine

This is a stone with a natural shimmer, so it's a great option for prosperity and luck spells. In fact, many people consider green aventurine to be the luckiest of all stones. It has the kind of luck that brings happiness and optimism, a wealth of positivity. Green aventurine's optimism helps stretch boundaries and reframe worldviews so that you can make your own luck. Use green aventurine in poppet spells for luck, especially when trying something new and expanding your horizons.

Keywords

- Prosperity
- Luck
- Abundance
- Healing

Hematite

If you hold hematite in your hand, it's heavier than it looks. This is a strong grounding stone containing iron, giving you a firm foundation. With hematite, you are acting from a grounded place of strength. Hematite offers support and protection. This stone's earthy feel also has the benefit of calming the mind, so use it in a poppet spell to relieve anxiety and encourage emotional stability.

Keywords

- Grounding
- Protection
- Strength
- Stability

Lapis Lazuli

This "stone of heaven" is really a stone of wisdom. Its intense blue hue reminds me of a clear blue sky, the kind of sky that allows you to see clearly. Lapis lazuli stimulates the third eye, perhaps unveiling hidden spiritual truths. Lapis lazuli has also been associated with dispelling headaches. This crystal sets the tone for clear communication and thereby strengthens friendships. Use it in poppet spells where clarity and specificity of intent are paramount, or when conferring that clarity and intent to someone else.

Keywords

- Wisdom
- Spiritual insight
- Communication
- Intuition

Moonstone

Find your inner light with this remarkable stone. If you look into a piece of moonstone, you can see that it is made up of tiny refractions. Its structure allows it to glow with innumerable lights from within—look closely and you'll see the lights within the light. This reflects the stone's association with intuition. Its luminescence reflects your inner light and illuminates the path to centered emotional balance. It's a stone of feminine energy and is associated with the moon, tides, and goddesses. Moonstone is great in poppet spells for recentering in the midst of chaos.

Keywords

- Feminine energy
- Intuition
- Balance

Rose Quartz

Use rose quartz for unconditional love. This is the compassion crystal, so use it to promote harmony between family members, friends, and romantic partners. It's a beautiful stone for emotional healing, especially when the person being healed was injured by someone close to them. It represents harmony and unity. Use rose quartz in a poppet healing spell and let it envelop your intent in the love and peace of the universe.

Keywords

- Love
- Compassion
- Healing
- Harmony

Selenite

Imagine a shower of stars above your head raining light down upon you, blessing you, purifying you, and connecting you to the spirit realm. This is the power of selenite. Selenite is a stone that is known for clearing the crown chakra and for cleansing negative spiritual energy. Not only does selenite connect you to the spiritual plane, it also connects you to the earthly realm, and specifically to others who recognize the light in you. It promotes camaraderie, pure friendship, and human connection.

Keywords

- Cleansing
- Purification
- Clarity
- Connection to higher realms

Tiger's Eye

If you are looking for courage and confidence, then this is the stone for you. Tiger's eye is a metamorphic rock; pressure, heat, and time can change normal, everyday rocks into this stand-out stone. Use tiger's eye in poppet spells for perseverance, fortitude, or dealing with problems head on.

Keywords

- Courage
- Confidence
- Manifestation
- Protection

These are just a few of the hundreds of crystals that you could use in poppet magick. Remember that stones should be selected based on your intention and the specific poppet's purpose. Always trust your intuition and personal connection with the stones. Choose crystals that resonate with you and your desired outcome.

Graveyard Dirt

Some people like to use magickal blessed sand or dirt as an ingredient in their poppet magick. Sand and dirt always add substance to poppets because of their grounding, earthy energies. Dirt and sand can be used according to their attributes; for example, sand can be used for its malleability and dirt for its solidity. They can also be used as a link to a certain location. Graveyard dirt is a particularly nice ingredient in poppet magick because it comes from sacred and holy ground. It also contains the energy of all the spirits at that site. However, there are many considerations when it comes to correctly sourcing graveyard dirt.

Gathering and using graveyard dirt is a process. It's essential to approach this process with respect, sensitivity, and a deep understanding of cultural and personal beliefs. Here are some guidelines to keep in mind if you choose to collect graveyard dirt for any magickal purpose.

Legal and Ethical Considerations

Before collecting graveyard dirt, ensure that you are legally allowed to do so. Some cemeteries have rules and regulations prohibiting the removal of materials. It's crucial to respect these guidelines in both the physical and spiritual world, so keep to the rules of the cemetery and always obtain spiritual permission. Enter with respect, knowing that you are entering sacred ground.

A good rule of thumb to know whether or not you are crossing an ethical line is to listen to your inner voice. If you feel like you are crossing an ethical line based on your own belief system, then you probably are. For example, there are some graves of famous people whose families and estates have asked that they not be disturbed in any way. Obviously, graves of the recently deceased with family members who frequently visit them are not a good choice. Collection of cemetery dirt should be done in a respectful, purposeful, discreet, and focused way.

Lastly, gathering cemetery dirt is a part of your spellwork. It's a sort of pilgrimage that should be done in person and with intent.

Seek Permission and Show Respect

If you choose to collect graveyard dirt, seek permission from the spiritual guardian of the graveyard. The spiritual keeper of the graveyard is the first person buried there. You may not be able to find that grave, but their spirit can be called upon to ask permission.

As you enter, energetically ask who the spiritual guardian is. You may not receive a name, but you will have gotten their attention. Energetically ask permission to remove a small amount of dirt from the graveyard. You will be able to tell that you have gotten permission by trusting your intuition. Your request to the spiritual guardian shows respect to the spirits and energies present in the cemetery.

Choose the Right Grave

If you have spiritually received permission to collect graveyard dirt, find a grave that resonates with your intention or the energy you wish to work with. This could be the grave of someone who embodied qualities or attributes that align with your magickal purpose. For example, if you are making a money poppet, try to find the headstone of the wealthiest person interred there. If you are making a love poppet, look for the graves of a couple who were buried next to each other. If you are doing a protection poppet, you might want to find the grave of a policeman or a decorated soldier. Trust your intuition and discernment when selecting a grave.

When you find an appropriate grave, ask for permission from the person buried there. If possible, speak out loud—sound has power. If you can't speak loudly, then whisper. For example, when addressing the spirits of a couple who were buried together while preparing a love poppet, you may say something like "I see that you were married for many years. Congratulations! May I have some dirt from your graves to perform a magickal love spell?" The spirits will hear you. Trust your intuition to tell you their answer. In other words, you will feel their agreement. Most spirits are happy to help, at least in my experience.

Gathering Dirt

After you have received permission from a spirit, leave an offering of flowers, coins, crystals, or at least a prayer. Then, it is time to gather your graveyard dirt. Take a spoonful or two of dirt—that's all you need. Place it in a clean container that is dedicated solely for this purpose. For the sake of potency and focused intent, I keep the graveyard dirt I have retrieved in an individual small, sealable bag or container made of glass, ceramic, or cloth until I use it in the poppet spell for which it was collected.

Be Discreet and Maintain Privacy

While collecting graveyard dirt, it's important to be discreet and respectful. Respect the privacy of any others in the graveyard. Avoid drawing unnecessary attention to yourself or disturbing the cemetery environment. This is sacred ground—it's holy land. Engage in this process with reverence and maintain a peaceful, quiet demeanor. Remember to do everything with permission and respect.

These guidelines are general suggestions. The specific practices and beliefs surrounding the collection of graveyard dirt vary among cultures and traditions. It's essential to research the cultural context and folklore associated with graveyard dirt in the specific magickal system you follow. If you are unsure about collecting graveyard dirt, or if you are uncomfortable with the process, consider alternative magickal materials or practices that align with your intentions. For example, you could use sand from a local playground where you have wonderful memories or dirt from a school campus for wisdom.

Chapter 14

Taglocking Your Poppet

To enhance the sympathetic link between your poppet and an individual, you must personalize it. This makes the magick stronger and more effective. If you are the target of your poppet magick, you must strengthen the bond between you and the poppet by personalizing it. If your focus is someone other than yourself, you must strengthen the bond between your poppet and the target by personalizing it specifically for them.

Poppets are often personalized by adding features that remind you of the target. You can draw or paint facial features on your poppet, for example. You could decorate the poppet with icing or markers, or you can go the extra mile by adding three-dimensional objects such as threat or felt. Give the poppet hair, button eyes, clothing, or other decorative items that are facsimiles of items belonging to the targeted individual. The more similar the poppet is to the person, the more powerful the sympathetic link between the two. This brings me to taglocking.

Taglocking

Taglocking is an optional but recommended practice in poppet personalization. It involves gathering actual personal items or belongings of the target individual, then attaching those items to the poppet; I'll share some examples later in this chapter. Taglocking is recommended because it helps establish a stronger connection between the poppet and the person it represents, amplifying the effectiveness of the spell or intention.

A taglock can help ensure that the energy and intention of the spell are directed toward the intended target. It adds a personal and unique element to the poppet, allowing for a more focused and tailored approach. Taglocks are symbolic representations of the person or situation, acting as a direct link to their energy. For example, you could gather a strand of hair or a thread of clothing from someone who is ill as part of a healing poppet. Once the poppet is charged, this becomes a conduit between the healing energy you are sending and the energy of the sick person. The taglock helps create a stronger connection and facilitates the desired outcome of the spell.

Why are taglocks so powerful? Well, a taglock contains something that is intimately connected to the target, thereby establishing a strong sympathetic link. A taglock is the heartbeat, the very essence that connects your magickal intentions to the universe and to the target. I've found that taglocking creates magickal conduits or keys that unlock doors to deeper, more effective magick.

Taglock Ethics

If you are not the intended target of your poppet magick, there are ethics that you should consider before taglocking. Using a taglock involves working with the personal energy of another individual. This raises ethical concerns, as the work may infringe upon their privacy and autonomy. It is important to respect the boundaries and rights of others when practicing spellwork.

If done incorrectly, taglocking can be seen as a form of energetic manipulation, especially when it involves working with someone's personal energy without their knowledge or consent. It is crucial to respect the free will and agency of others when engaging in any spellwork.

When making a poppet for someone else, I always ask for permission. I believe getting consent from the target leads to the creation of a more powerful poppet. Ask, "Can I make a poppet for you?" Respect the person's answer one way or another. You may need to explain what a poppet is. Then, explain the spell that you have in mind and ask for a taglock item.

Most of the time, the target will get excited that you want to do something good for them, and this will also increase the efficacy of the spell.

Of course, asking permission does depend on the kind of spellwork you're planning. You can't get permission from someone who is in a coma, for example, even if the work is well intentioned. You also aren't going to ask permission to do a binding or banishing. When deciding whether or not to do work without another's permission, let your moral compass guide you.

Taglocks work on a principle that transcends the physical realm. They connect your intentions to the spiritual essence of the person, creating a link that is both mystical and profound. This connection allows your magick to be focused, direct, and powerful. This small yet mighty item is what breathes life into your poppet's purpose, making it a key element in your magickal toolkit.

Approach taglocking with mindfulness, integrity, and respect for the well-being and autonomy of the targeted person. When taglocking, consider all of the ethical implications and ensure that your intentions are in alignment with positive and responsible magickal practices. Also consider the potential consequences of your actions to ensure that your intentions align with your principles. Remember, the energy you send into the universe returns to you magnified. It's a bridge, a link between your will and the cosmic energies that catalyze magick into action. Always operate within the boundaries of harmlessness and respect for free will.

Choosing Your Taglock

The closer the connection your taglock has to the person, the stronger your poppet's influence. Taglocks physically connect the target and the poppet. Selecting a taglock is an important part of the process. It requires intuition, thoughtfulness, and a deep connection to the energies you're working with. Here are some of my favorite taglock options.

Locks of Hair or Nail Clippings

Hair and nail clippings are considered very potent taglocks because they are part of the person's body. They carry the essence of the target and create a strong, direct link.

Personal Belongings

Personal items like a piece of clothing, jewelry, or anything frequently used or worn by the target hold their energy and can work wonders as a taglock. Objects like a favorite pen or a cherished book are also imbued with the person's energy. They hold memories and emotions, making them excellent taglocks.

Handwriting Samples

There's magick in the written word, especially when it's penned by the person you're focusing on.

Photographs

A picture of the target, particularly a recent one, is like a mirror reflecting the person's essence.

Bodily Fluids

Saliva, blood, or other bodily fluids are extremely powerful because they come from the body, just like hair and nail clippings. However, these are less commonly used due to both ethical and health concerns. Your magick should always be in harmony with your moral compass.

Audio Recordings or Videos

In our modern era, a snippet of someone's voice or a video can serve as a dynamic taglock, pulsating with the person's energy. For the technologically inclined, you can save an audio recording or video on a flash drive and stuff it inside the poppet. If you do use technology as part of your poppet creation, don't bury or burn the poppet, as those methods are reserved for poppets made of natural materials.

Footprints or Handprints

A footprint or handprint is a unique mark that carries the physical touch of a person. Either can add a personal dimension to your poppet magick.

No Physical Taglocks Available?

You may not have access to any items to personalize your poppet. Let's say you're making a poppet for someone and they happen to be located somewhere else, or you are making a poppet for a banishing or binding. If you don't have access to any personal items, you can instead add the target's full name and birthday (if known), as well as symbols that represent the person. For example, if the person always wears a ball cap with their favorite team's logo, create or draw a ball cap on the poppet. Make the poppet look like the target as you see them.

Attaching Taglocks with Intent

Attaching the chosen taglock(s) to your poppet is a creative and intentional act. Your focus is crucial. There are numerous methods of attachment. In this section, I will share the most common methods of attaching taglocks. Of course, methods will vary depending on the type of item and the nature of the poppet. Regardless of the method you choose, attachment will add layers of meaning and power to your spellwork. Each action should be deliberate and filled with purpose.

Sewing

Some items, like hair clippings or taglocks made of cloth, can be sewn into the poppet.

Stuffing

If the poppet is hollow, taglocks can be stuffed inside.

Creating a Pocket

If the poppet is not hollow, create a small pocket (sewn, glued, or otherwise affixed to the poppet) to house the taglock. Doing so can be symbolic of keeping the person's essence safe and nurtured.

Glueing

Glueing is perfect for paper-based taglocks or photographs. As the glue binds the taglock to the poppet, visualize your intentions being firmly set.

Tying

Items such as a piece of jewelry can be tied around the poppet with ribbon or string. You can use this method to symbolize that the bond between poppet and target cannot be broken.

Weaving

For those who are adept with needle and thread, you might try embroidering the taglock into your poppet.

Natural Wrapping

You can use natural materials, like vines or twigs, to encase the taglock and wrap it onto the poppet. This adds the extra element of earth magick.

Your Own Personal Poppet

Creating a personal poppet to represent yourself can be a meaningful and powerful tool for many purposes, including self-reflection, intention setting, and self-empowerment. It's fun to personalize or taglock your own doll. I always add my name on the back along with personal items to really make it my own.

You can create a personal poppet for a specific intent, or you can create a general poppet that can be used for anything you need along the way. I have a personal general-purpose poppet on hand for needs as they arise. One day I sprained my knee, so I put a poultice wrap and some special herbs around my poppet's knee with the intention of healing faster. I also stuck some pins in my poppet's knee to work like acupuncture needles. After doing my poppet magick, I truly felt healing energy going to my knee. Poppets really will assist you in manifesting healing of any kind.

For example, if you are concerned about your knee like I was, you could draw little hearts on your poppet's knee just to give it a little more love and attention. There's no right or wrong way to do poppet magick; it's all about your intent and how you can visualize it.

If you do poppet magick for yourself, you will also feel it working. After all, the doll is representing you. To create a poppet for yourself, use the standard methods shared in chapters 9 and 10. When you are done, take a moment to hold the poppet in your hands. Connect to it and infuse it with your energy. You can state affirmations, blessings, or personal intentions to empower the poppet as a representation of yourself.

When I created my personal poppet, I created it with a lot of different herbs and ingredients that had personal significance to me. I claimed the poppet by saying, "I name you Patti Negri. I name you. You are representing me. This is your birthday. You are going to keep me protected."

Remember, this poppet is a deeply personal creation that represents you. Adapt the process, materials, and decorations to align with your unique personality and intentions. Then, keep the poppet in a special place, carry it with you, or use it during rituals or meditations as a tool for self-reflection, empowerment, and intention setting.

A Final Whisper of Wisdom

Taglocks are the secret ingredients that transform a simple poppet into a powerful magickal ally. Taglocking links the physical world with the mystical, carrying our intentions to the universe. Let your heart and intuition guide you in the choice and use of taglocks. Embrace the responsibility that comes with this powerful form of magick. When done right, the art of using taglocks can bring about transformative changes, healing, and blessings. So, gather your taglocks, weave your intentions, and let the magick flow through your hands.

Chapter 15

Working with Your Poppet

Congratulations on creating your poppet! Now that you've successfully completed the "art part," personalized your poppet, and added taglocks, it's time to start working with your poppet. This is the part where you pour spiritual energy into your creation and manifest your magick.

In this chapter, I'll cover the enspiriting process. *Enspiriting* is another word for charging your poppet with your intent. It should be noted that when you enspirit a poppet, you are *not* creating a haunted doll. You are *not* calling a disembodied, sentient spirit into a doll. Instead, you are calling upon the forces of the universe. You are using your magick and the power of the cosmos to channel spiritual energy, powering-up your poppet with your intention. In short, you're putting your thoughts into action with a purposeful magickal object: your poppet.

I will also cover how to use your poppet and where to keep it. After all, you've made and charged a magickal object! Now that it's imbued with your magick and is a part of your magickal toolkit, you have to take care of it, at least until you're ready to dispose of it. At the end of this chapter, you'll learn how to have a funeral for your poppet, which will disperse your magick and dispel it back into the universe. I've included a beautiful ritual that can be very peaceful and satisfying, even if you spent a lot of time creating the perfect poppet.

Charging a Poppet

Enspiriting or charging a poppet is not the same as inviting a spirit into a haunted doll. Haunted dolls are vessels for independent spirits or entities. Enspiriting a poppet refers to the act of filling the creation with spiritual energy. Think of it like charging a battery. You are charging the poppet with the energy of the universe for a specific purpose. A poppet does not have free will—it exists to do *your* will.

Exercise
Charging Your Poppet

Here's a general method for enspiriting or charging a poppet. In this exercise, you will be connecting your poppet to the energy of the universe by passing it through your energy. You are literally charging the poppet.

Supplies

- Your poppet
- A sacred space
- Blessed water, essential oil such as lavender, or incense such as sandalwood, frankincense, or myrrh

Preparation

The first step is to set your intention. This may be the thirtieth time you are reading this, but nothing is more important than setting your intention. Determine the specific purpose or desired outcome you want to infuse into the poppet, and focus on it.

Next, prepare a sacred space for your ritual. If you need more instructions, see chapter 10.

Directions

Focus and clear your mind. Then, pray, meditate, or visualize connecting to the divine power of the universe. You can also call on the divine energy that resonates with your intention.

Once you are in a place where you have connected with a universal higher energy, call upon deities, spiritual guides, or guardians that align with you and with your purpose. Ask for their presence, guidance, and assistance so you can infuse the poppet with energy and intention.

Now, it's time to charge your poppet and do some magick with a personal energy transfer. Hold the poppet in your hands and close your eyes. Focus on your own energy and intention. Visualize your energy flowing from your hands into the poppet, infusing it with your intention and aligning it with the divine energy you have invoked.

Speak your intentions out loud. Speak what it is you want from the universe, and speak who you want it for. For example, you could say, "This poppet will represent me, my health, and my life," or "This healing poppet will represent and support my mother as she goes through surgery."

State your intention clearly, and don't forget to express gratitude for the divine assistance you've invoked. If you have specific affirmations or prayers that resonate with your intention or are important to your belief system, speak them now.

Next, hold the poppet up to your mouth and breathe your intention into it. Your breath is your life force, your pneuma.

Perform symbolic actions that further enhance the enspiriting process. This could include sprinkling the poppet with sacred water or essential oil, or passing it through incense smoke, to purify and bless it.

Now, you will seal the poppet. Hold the poppet close to your heart and visualize it being enveloped in a vibrant, glowing energy. Visualize this energy sealing and protecting the poppet, imbuing it with the spiritual essence and intention you have set.

Finally, express your gratitude. Thank any deities, spiritual guides, or guardians that you called upon for their presence and assistance. Then, express gratitude for the enspirited poppet and its purpose.

Close the ritual space in a way that is meaningful to you. You can say a closing prayer or offer a token of appreciation to the guardians. You may choose to say, "So mote it be," "Amen," or "So shall it be."

Remember, the enspiriting process can be customized according to your beliefs and practices. It's important to approach it with reverence, focus, and a clear intention. Trust your intuition and follow the guidance of your spiritual path as you enspirit your poppet.

Poppet Acupuncture

Using pins can help direct and focus energy in your enspirited poppet. I often use this technique in my work, and it's excellent. Even though people might have a negative perspective of this practice, pins really can help with healing—think of it like acupuncture. If I feel a headache coming on, I will get my personal poppet and put a pin or two in its head. If I've got a head cold, I'll put pins into where my sinuses would be on the doll. If I have chest congestion, I will put a pin into my poppet's chest. With an upset stomach, I'll put a pin into my poppet's belly. You get the idea.

I like to use sewing pins with the different colored round heads. That way, I can coordinate the pinhead color with the kind of magick that I am doing. For example, I use blue pins for healing, red pins for passion, and green pins for money.

Another nice technique is to use pins when you want to get rid of something, whether that is illness, negative thoughts, or a bad habit. I put pins in the area that is connected to what I want to release. Then, each day for the next several days, I remove one pin for the healing going on. You can use pins for a variety of ailments and unhealthy habits. For example, say you are choosing to quit smoking over the next week. Put seven pins in the part of your poppet where the lungs would be. Every day over the next week, remove one pin with the intention that the pin represents your desire to smoke and you are removing that desire. You are also affirming your intention and commitment to not smoke with each removal. When all the pins are removed, your desire to smoke should be eliminated.

Get creative. There are endless ways you can work with pins.

Burn or Bury

Some traditions and practices burn or bury their poppets once they are made. In this way, they are literally sending their wishes and magick up to the universe or planting it in the ground.

If you would like to burn or bury, take into consideration the health of the environment. If you are in a drought, for example, burning is not a good choice. Only use biodegradable materials when you bury a poppet. If you choose to burn, only use natural materials that are safe to burn. Don't bury or burn a poppet that incorporates plastics, for example. Another consideration is that if you bury a poppet and then want to reverse or cancel the spell for some reason, you must remember where it was buried in order to dig it up. And, of course, this won't be an option with a burned poppet.

If you choose to bury or burn your poppet, you should set your intention before beginning. You could say something like, "I've made this beautiful poppet, and now I'm sending it [up into the universe, down into the earth]."

Be careful with these methods. Engage in the process safely, and make sure you choose an out-of-the-way space where your poppet won't be disturbed. I have had one of my poppets dug up by a dog before.

Storing the Poppet

Since I like to have a physical, tangible representation of the work I am doing, I personally like to keep my poppets around and accessible until they are finished. I rarely burn or bury my poppets.

I often keep my poppets on my altar while working with them. If your space doesn't allow for you to have a permanent magickal altar, you can keep your poppet safe on any special shelf or table. If your poppet is part of a protection spell, put the poppet in a box and place it under your bed or tuck it away in a drawer. Conversely, if your poppet is part of a specific spell and helps you focus your intent, you may choose a location that reminds you of it, such as leaving a health poppet by your gym bag. You might want to enhance the work by placing salt or other protective items around it. In that case, wrap those items with the poppet in a black or white cloth and then tuck the poppet safely away.

Wherever your poppet is stored, ensure it is somewhere your pets or kids can't get ahold of it. Rest assured, if a dog does manage to take a bite out of your poppet, the recipient of the spell is not going to lose a limb like in the movie *The Witches of Eastwick*. On a similar note, if you use poppets for baneful magick (which I personally do not) and you rip the arm off the poppet, it doesn't mean the arm of the person you targeted will get ripped off. It might seem obvious, but magick doesn't work like that.

Regardless of your preferred outcome, you will want to keep your poppet safe from damage. Here are some things to consider while determining where to keep your poppet.

- **Personal Preference:** The placement of a poppet can vary based on personal preference and the specific purpose of the doll. Some people choose to keep their poppets on their altars or in a sacred space dedicated to their spiritual practice. Others prefer to keep them hidden away in a safe and private place.
- **Intention and Purpose:** Consider the intention and purpose of your poppet when deciding where to keep it. For example, if the poppet is intended for protection, you may choose to keep it near

the entrance of your home or in a space where you spend a significant amount of time.

- **Energetic Considerations:** Consider the energy of the space where you plan to keep the poppet. It's generally beneficial to choose a clean and energetically harmonious environment. Avoid placing the poppet in areas with excessive clutter or negative energy.
- **Safety and Privacy:** Ensure that the poppet is kept in a safe and secure location, especially if it contains personal items or materials that could be harmful if mishandled. Consider privacy concerns as well, especially if the poppet represents someone else or involves personal information.

Do what feels right to you. Ultimately, the decision of where to keep your poppet should align with your intentions, beliefs, and personal practices. Listen to your intuition and choose a space that feels right for you and your magickal work.

Funeral for a Poppet

You will know when you are finished with a poppet. When you got what you were looking for, or you no longer want what a poppet was doing for you, the spell is done and finished: You found the love you wanted, you are healthy, you stopped whatever you were doing, or you just don't need the poppet anymore. Now, you must properly dispose of it.

The first thing you should do is thank the poppet. You could say, "I thank you for your help. I thank you for the magick that you've done." Next, say, "I separate now and forever from this poppet. It no longer represents sympathetic magick for myself [or the name of the person it was made for]." After you have spoken these sentences aloud, cleanse the poppet with salt, incense smoke, water, or sunlight. This will release the poppet from its task.

Once the poppet is cleansed, you should completely disassemble it. Take out the stitching, the stuffing, and the ingredients. Take it completely apart—you want to take all the energy out of it. Then and only then can you burn it, bury it, or even throw it away.[23] You can even allow the elements to lead your disposal. If you want more flow in your life, use a water method. If you feel the need for grounding, incorporate the earth element by burying it. If you want some energy or passion, choose burning.

Finally, you should perform a ritualistic disposal of the poppet to release its energy and intention. I call this a poppet funeral. This can be

23. Note: If your poppet contains or is made from nonbiodegradable or potentially harmful materials, such as synthetic fabrics, chemicals, or sharp objects, it is important to dispose of them responsibly. Check local guidelines and follow appropriate methods for safely disposing of such materials.

done in various ways, depending on your personal beliefs and practices. Here are a few methods to consider.

Exercise
Burying Ritual

This exercise involves burying a poppet in the earth to return its energy to nature. Only choose this method if your poppet is biodegradable. Be mindful not to put anything toxic or unnatural into the ground, especially around plants, gardens, or areas people or children frequent.

Supplies

- Your poppet
- A shovel

Directions

Pick a spot that feels right, both as a location and a place for a poppet to decompose.

Disassemble the poppet as much as possible before burying. Remove anything that is not biodegradable. Thank the poppet for a job well done as you disassemble.

Dig a hole with focus and respect. Then, bury the remains.

Thank the earth for taking the poppet's energy in and transmuting it. Release your connection to the poppet and let go. Say something out loud, like "I release you."

Exercise
Burning Ritual

You can burn a poppet in a ceremonial fire to transform its energy. Fire is sacred and powerful, so be sure to use it safely. Only burn a poppet if the material is natural and safe to burn, and be careful to avoid any fumes or smoke that might be toxic. This method is best done outside.

Supplies

- Firesafe container big enough to burn your poppet in
- Your poppet
- Matches or a lighter

Directions

Build an environmentally safe fire in your container. When the flames are big enough to envelop the poppet, toss the poppet in with respect and gratitude.

Thank the poppet for a job well done.

Watch as the fire releases the poppet's energy as it burns. See the smoke release it into the atmosphere.

When the poppet has burned to ash, use words of power to release the spell and let go. If you are left with stones, crystals, or metal, bury them.

Other Funeral Methods

The most important thing about poppet disposal is to do all things respectfully and in alignment with your beliefs and practices. Consider the ethical, environmental, and personal implications of your chosen disposal method.

Trust your intuition and follow your personal spiritual path when it comes to letting go of a poppet after you have finished working with it. Here are two more ways to say goodbye.

Water Release

If your poppet is biodegradable, you can immerse it in flowing water to cleanse and release its energy. Be very careful to remove any items that will upset the ecosystem or wildlife—good magick is magick that works with and respects Mother Nature.

Find a flowing river, stream, or ocean. Disassemble the poppet as much as possible, unless you created a paper poppet. Watch as the poppet is taken by the water. Release and let go.

Symbolic Disposal

You can dispose of the poppet symbolically. This involves dismantling or deconstructing the poppet in a respectful manner, separating its components, and then discarding them individually. For example, you can remove any personal items or taglocks and return them to the person they represented. Once you have finished discarding the pieces of the poppet, release and let go.

Recycling Poppets

Can you reuse a poppet? Personally, I do not reuse poppets. Each one is a specific spell. I make a new poppet every time I want to do poppet magick unless I am working with my general poppet, which I dress and adjust as needed.

If you want to reuse or recycle a poppet, first do a deep cleansing of the doll, clearing it of its original purpose. You don't want any mixed messages sent out! I recommend performing an entire ritual where you thank the poppet for its original work and then release it, similar to the funeral exercises shared in this chapter. Then, thoroughly cleanse the poppet using one of the techniques in chapter 9. I recommend letting the cleansed poppet rest for an entire moon cycle (from the new moon to the full moon and back to the dark moon) before repurposing it.

Part III
Poppet Spells and Recipes

CHAPTER 16

Spells and Recipes

In this chapter, you'll find three different kinds of poppet recipes: classic poppets, biodegradable poppets, and food-based poppets. I have also included some basic customizable spells. When you reach the spells section, know that whatever poppet works for you is the best poppet to use. All spells can be used with any style of poppet.

As I stated at the beginning of chapter 9, poppets can be made as a long-lasting arts and crafts project, or they can be made to be immediately burned or buried. There are a wide range of options. Here is a brief overview of what you will find in the coming pages.

The Classic Poppets

The first set of poppet recipes are classics. These are what you might expect in a poppet recipe. I included options for sewing and no-sew poppets. You can make many of the classic poppets biodegradable if you so choose.

The Biodegradable Poppets

If you intend to create an environmentally safe poppet that can be left in nature, it's important to use biodegradable and eco-friendly materials. It is essential to be mindful of the environment and choose materials that will not harm nature when buried, burned, or thrown away.

Nature makes some of the easiest materials to work with. The cheapest and easiest material is mud. You may have played in it as a kid, and now you can use those skills as an adult. You can find mud in your own backyard, if applicable, or you can get some hydroponic planting mix at your local garden center. Other easy biodegradable poppets can be made from moss, twigs, leaves, flowers, herbs, popsicle sticks, or any combination of these items. If you are a skilled woodworker, then use those techniques. Do you have access to shells and driftwood? You could use those materials; they would make a lovely poppet.

The best part about biodegradable poppets is that they will decompose and easily return to the earth when you're done with them. With some mindfulness, you can create an environmentally safe poppet that can be left in nature without causing harm.

The Food-Based Poppets

If you're not into the great outdoors but still want something biodegradable, consider food-based poppets. Food-based poppets are also an excellent way to get a stuffable doll form for those who are not crafty. In fact, if you have access to premade dough, edible poppet recipes may be the absolute best way to create a poppet fast. I've included some premade dough recipes and ones you can make from scratch.

Food-based poppets are mostly carbohydrate based and can include gingerbread people, biscuits, and traditional bread baby poppets, like those offered at grave sites on All Saints' Day in some cultures in South America.

To be clear, not all food-based poppets are meant for consumption. Whether they can be consumed depends on the taglocks and other ingredients you use to stuff the poppet. In the food-based poppet recipes I have included, only the French bread poppet is edible.

Poppets Spells by Need

At the end of this chapter, you'll find a number of handy spells and correspondences for specific intentions that I have used and taught in my classes. I've found them to be effective and a great foundation for poppet magick. The spells I have included use the classic poppet style and list suggested ingredients for example purposes. However, you can use another poppet form and/or different ingredients. Do what feels right for you.

Please remember that everything shared in this chapter is a guideline. You can always put your own spin on things by swapping the materials, etc. The power is yours.

Classic

Basic Poppet

This poppet is one of the most popularly used styles these days. I call it a gingerbread poppet because of its shape. This is the classic sewn poppet, though it can also be glued.

If you choose to sew the poppet, you can use whatever stitch you like. I use the same whip stitch I learned as a seven-year-old Brownie to get my merit badge. Whatever stitch you use—whip stitch, straight stitch, running stitch, or even your sewing machine—the point is to secure your poppet ingredients. There are no merit badges for how neatly you do it.

Not in a sewing mood? You still have options. If you are handier with glue or a stapler, follow your bliss! Modify the supply list as needed.

Creating a gingerbread-style poppet can be a delightful way to infuse your intentions with a touch of sweetness. Here's a step-by-step guide to making a basic poppet.

Supplies

- Two identically sized pieces of felt or fabric or one piece folded in half (I find two 12" × 12" felt squares or one 12" × 24" piece to be a workable size)
- Scissors
- Pen or fabric marker
- Sewing needle and thread
- Stuffing material such as cotton balls or dried herbs
- Embroidery thread or thin string, any color (optional)
- Sewing pins or safety pins (optional)
- Decorative items such as buttons, ribbons, etc. (optional)
- Taglocking items (optional)

Directions

1. Start by drawing the shape of a gingerbread person on one piece of felt or fabric (or on the facing side if you've doubled it).

2. Draw a ¼ inch outline around the figure you've just drawn. This is your cut line.
3. Once you're satisfied with your sketch, hold the two pieces of fabric together (or the doubled piece). If you are using sewing or safety pins, pin the pieces of cloth together so they don't slip while you're cutting.
4. Using a scissors, cut out the shape on the cutline. Be sure to cut through both layers of the fabric.
5. Stitch the back and the front of your poppet together between the cut line and the poppet outline, leaving a small opening on one side so you can stuff the poppet with ingredients. If you want to hide the seams, you can turn your poppet inside out now.
6. Now, it's time to decorate the poppet. Be creative and add any personal touches you desire. You can use fabric markers or embroidery thread to create body details, facial features, and other decorative elements. If you would like to add any objects like buttons, ribbons, sequins, or beads, you can glue or sew them onto the poppet to enhance its appearance. Make sure to attach them securely.
7. Consider adding a small pouch or pocket to the front or back of the poppet. This pocket can hold specific herbs, crystals, or

written intentions related to your magickal working. It could also hold ingredients that may be too bulky to stuff. If you would like to add a pocket, simply cut out a smaller piece of fabric in a contrasting color, fold and secure the edges, and then sew, staple, or glue it onto the poppet.

8. Once you have finished decorating the poppet, it's time to stuff it. Fill the poppet with your chosen stuffing material, such as cotton balls or dried herbs. You could add taglocking items to give it a plump and three-dimensional shape. Be careful not to fill the poppet entirely: Leave enough space to allow for flexibility and easy closure.
9. After filling the poppet, seal the opening by folding the edges of the fabric together. Sew it, staple it, or glue it shut, securing the stuffing inside the poppet.
10. If desired, you can attach a loop of string or embroidery thread to the top of the poppet to serve as a hanger or a way to easily carry the poppet with you.
11. Charge your poppet using the instructions provided in chapter 15.

And there you have it—a gingerbread-style classic poppet! This charming creation can be used in spellwork or meditation, or it can simply be a decorative item in your sacred space. Enjoy infusing it with your intentions and magickal energy.

Classic

No-Sew Poppet

Here is a simple do-it-yourself poppet that requires no sewing whatsoever.

Supplies

- Piece of fabric or cloth, preferably a natural material like cotton (could be a piece of old clothing from you or whomever the poppet is for)
- Ruler
- Scissors
- Stuffing material such as cotton balls or dried herbs
- String, yarn, or embroidery thread
- Pen or fabric marker (optional)
- Taglocking items (optional)

Directions

1. Begin by choosing the fabric for your poppet. Then, cut the fabric into a rectangle. The size of the rectangle should depend on the desired size of the poppet; at least 8.5" × 14" will work for most people. You will be folding this fabric in half to make both the front and back half of your poppet.
2. Lay the rectangle flat on a surface, with the shorter side in front of you. Using a ruler, measure the long side of the rectangle and find its halfway point. Then, draw a straight line all the way across the cloth. Your rectangle should now appear to be divided into a top half and a bottom half.
3. Mark the center point of the dividing line. This point should also be the center of the rectangle.
4. On the bottom half of the rectangle—the half closest to you—you are going to draw your poppet. The top of the poppet's head should touch the center point of the rectangle. Use a pen or fabric marker to draw the outline of the poppet's body.
5. Once you are finished drawing your poppet, fold your fabric in half on the dividing line. Fold it so that your poppet outline is facing you.
6. Begin to cut along the drawn outline of the poppet using scissors. Make sure you are cutting through both layers of fabric at once.

When you get near the top of the poppet's head, stop cutting. Do not cut all the way around the poppet's head—allow some space around the center point to remain. When you open up the cloth, the two sides should be connected at the head.

7. Once you have the fabric shape, front and back, you can start decorating the poppet if desired. You could use markers, fabric paint, or embroidery thread to add facial features, hair, or any other details you like. This step is optional but does enhance the poppet's appearance.
8. Next, it's time to fill the poppet with stuffing material. Start by placing small amounts of stuffing inside the poppet, starting with the limbs and then filling the body. You can use cotton balls, dried herbs, or any soft material you have available. Add enough filling so that the poppet is firm but flexible. Do not overstuff or you won't be able to close the poppet.
9. After you've filled the poppet, begin closing it by pressing the edges together and folding them over. Folding ensures that the stuffing won't come out as easily. Next, you are going to secure the folded edges by tying the poppet together in sections using string, thread, or yarn. I like to use embroidery thread because it ties neatly and comes in many colors.

10. I recommend beginning by tying the poppet at the neck. Carefully hold or lift the poppet, with each of its sides and its stuffing, and tie a tight knot around the neck using string, thread, or yarn. This knot will hold the two halves of the poppet together and keep the stuffing from spilling out.
11. After you've secured the neck, I recommend tying at the shoulders, then moving on to each arm. You may have to refold the edges as you go. Ultimately, where you tie is up to you. You could tie the poppet's shoulders, elbows, wrists, waist, hips, knees, and ankles, or you could just tie off the neck, ankles, and wrists and be done. It's up to you! It doesn't matter what your poppet looks like—all that matters is making it with intent and ensuring the stuffing is secured inside.
12. If desired, you can attach a loop of string or embroidery thread to the top of the poppet to serve as a hanger or a way to easily carry the poppet with you.
13. Charge your poppet using the instructions provided in chapter 15.

If folding the fabric in half and cutting the form is too crafty for you, you can always use a single layer of fabric. The only difference is that you'll have to glue on your ingredients rather than stuff the poppet.

Classic

Patti's Paper Napkin Poppet

This is my quick and easy paper napkin poppet. This poppet is easy to make, even for the craft challenged, and it is perfect for a poppet you want to safely dispose of. Paper napkin poppets are the ones I use most often when I want to dispose of my poppet in nature, since paper is biodegradable.

Supplies

- A square paper napkin
- String
- A marker or pen
- Herbs that work with your intent
- Essential oils that work with your intent
- Taglocking items (optional)

Directions

1. If the napkin is folded, fully open it. At the very center of the napkin, place a spoonful of herbs that align with your intention.
2. Gather the napkin in the middle and twist around the herbs to create a head. Then, use string to tie off the head.
3. Separate the four corners of the napkin, turning two into legs and two into arms. Twist or use string to tie off the limbs.
4. Draw eyes and a mouth on the head of your poppet. You can also draw hair if you'd like.
5. Anoint the poppet with corresponding essential oils.
6. Add an environmentally safe taglocking item, or write the target's name or initials on the doll as a taglock.
7. Charge your poppet using the instructions provided in chapter 15.

This poppet is biodegradable as long as all of your ingredients are organic and nontoxic. You may choose to dispose of biodegradable poppets by burying them, burning them, or releasing them in water. If you plan to dispose of your poppet by leaving it in water, consider attaching a stone to the bottom of the poppet to help it sink.

If even one of your ingredients was inorganic, disassemble the poppet to dispose of it. Then, see chapter 15 for disposal ideas.

Classic

Corn Dolly Poppet

Corn dollies have long been used in magick as harvest dolls. The harvest doll symbolizes the great harvest, the maiden, fertility, vitality, the natural cycle of life, and death and rebirth, much like the cycle of crops. If these attributes align with what you want your poppet to do, a corn dolly is a great choice.

This poppet is also biodegradable.

Supplies

- 5 corn husks
- Bucket of water
- Towel or paper towels
- Scissors
- Natural string or twine
- Taglocking items (optional)

Directions

1. Soak corn husks in water for at least ten minutes, then pat dry.
2. Trim away any uneven edges.
3. Use twine or string to tie two husks together, with the veins going vertically.
4. Roll a strip of husk into a ball. Insert taglocking items, if using.
5. Fold the tied husks over the ball and secure with twine to create the poppet's head. The long husks hanging down become the legs.
6. Roll a piece of husk into a cylinder and tie both ends to make the arms.
7. Insert the arms through the torso beneath the head and tie underneath, making the waist.
8. If you'd like, add a strip of husk to represent hair or a headpiece.
9. Charge your poppet using the directions in chapter 15.

You may choose to dispose of this biodegradable poppet by burying it, burning it, or releasing it in water. If you plan to dispose of your poppet by leaving it in water, consider attaching a stone to the bottom of the poppet to help it sink.

CLASSIC

Yarn or String Poppet

This is a simple poppet that almost anyone can make. You may recognize these as yarn dolls from country-themed stores or holiday fairs, sometimes called "yarn angels." You may have even made one as a child. Yarn, cardboard (or a journal), and scissors are all you need. You can use thin or thick yarn. Technically, you could even make one out of a mop. However, if you have numerous taglocking items, please make sure the yarn is plush enough (and tied tightly enough) to keep your items in place.

Supplies

- A stiff 6" × 9" piece of cardboard or a standard A5 journal
- A ball of yarn or string in a color that matches your intention or in white, which represents any color
- Scissors

- Small items you can insert into the head and/or body of the doll for extra intention and magick, such as crystals
- Taglocking items (optional)

Directions

1. The piece of cardboard/journal serves as your guide. First, cut a piece of yarn slightly longer than the length of the guide, about 11–12 inches long. Then, carefully place this piece of yarn at the top of the guide. Later, you'll use this yarn to tie the top of your poppet's head.
2. Hold the guide in your non-dominant hand, using your thumb to hold the end of the remaining ball of yarn against your guide. Using your dominant hand, wrap the yarn over the length of string at the top and back around the guide, creating one big loop.
3. Loop the yarn around the length of the guide over and over. The more you wrap, the wider your doll will be. You will need between twenty and sixty loops for a small doll.
4. When you are satisfied with the width of your doll, squish your loops together at the top of the guide. Tie the length of yarn from step one at the top to secure the poppet.

5. Carefully slide the loops from your guide. I recommend holding on to the tied portion at the top, which will be the crown of your poppet's head. Lay the poppet on a flat surface.
6. Cut a 3 inch piece of yarn. Then, tie that piece of yarn around the loops about an inch below the top, creating the head of your poppet. (Some people use embroidery thread for this, but yarn works just fine.)
7. Cut two 1½ inch pieces of yarn. Set aside.
8. Looking down at your poppet, pull aside a few loops on the left and an equal number of loops on the right. These separated loops will form the arms of your poppet. Tie the ends of the arms with the 1½ inch pieces of yarn. Then, trim the bottom of the loops off to create hands.
9. Cut another 3 inch piece of yarn. Tie the waist of your poppet below the arms.
10. You can decide whether you'd like your poppet to wear a skirt or pants. If you'd like it to wear a skirt, which is traditional for yarn poppets, you don't need to do anything else. You can trim the bottom of the loops to create more of a hem-like appearance. If you want the poppet to wear pants, halve the loops beneath the waist

to form legs. Tie each half near the ankle, then trim the bottom of the loops to create feet.

11. Add small crystals or items to the head or body for extra power. And, if you have taglocking items, insert them now.
12. Charge your poppet using the instructions provided in chapter 15.

These are cuddly little poppets you can carry with you, and they're small enough to fit most anywhere. To dispose of the poppet, disassemble it as outlined in chapter 15. If the yarn you used is natural and biodegradable, you can burn the poppet, bury it, or place it in water.

Classic

Poppet Made from a Doll

You can turn almost any commercial or store-bought doll into a magickal poppet if you so choose. Remember, thrift stores and secondhand shops are great places to find cheap dolls. I will say, smaller dolls tend to work better.

Supplies

- A small non-fabric doll with a removable head
- Herbs that correspond with the attributes you want your poppet to have
- Permanent marker
- Cleansing materials
- Taglocking items (optional)

Directions

1. Choose a doll that best represents you or the person you are making it for.
2. Cleanse the doll by doing a smoke cleansing, placing it in the moonlight, or another cleansing method. (See chapter 10 for techniques.) You want the poppet to start out "clear," whether it was store-bought, secondhand, or even a doll from your childhood.
3. Remove any clothes from the doll. Check to see if the head can be easily removed without breaking; many can.
4. Remove the head and fill it with corresponding herbs that fit your intention. Insert taglocking items if using. Put the head back on.
5. Using permanent marker, draw sigils or symbols on the body of the doll. Put these sigils on the main body of the doll, where they will be covered up when you redress the doll. You could draw a big heart on the chest for a love poppet or the Helm of Awe symbol for a protection poppet.
6. If possible, dress your doll in something that aligns with your intention or the spell you are creating. Even a small modification from what it was originally wearing could make a powerful impact if needed.
7. Charge your doll with your words, breath, and passionate intent. For further instructions on charging poppets, see chapter 15.

To dispose of the poppet, disassemble it as outlined in chapter 15.

Biodegradable

Mud Baby Poppet

This is a classic mud doll. Put on protective gardening gloves and sink your hands into some water and soil. Please choose seed-starting soil or another kind of soil that does not have manure in it.

Supplies

- Mud
- Wooden board
- Gardening gloves
- Stones
- Taglocking items (optional)

Directions

1. Play in the mud to create a ball. Put your mud ball onto an untreated wooden board, then begin to shape the mud

into a poppet form. You can create a humanlike shape or a simple form that represents your intention.

2. Place personalized items into your mud baby poppet if you are using them. Don't overfill your poppet with items or the mud will not hold together.
3. Add stones to represent the poppet's eyes and other features.
4. Now, let the mud dry out a bit. You want your poppet's form to harden somewhat. Timing will depend on the temperature and humidity of your area, as well as how much water retention the soil has. It's a waiting game, like watching water boil. This is the hard part.
5. Charge your poppet using the instructions provided in chapter 15.

Your poppet is biodegradable and can eventually be disposed of in water or be buried. If you plan to dispose of your poppet by leaving it in water, remember that it will immediately disintegrate. However, the idea is that it will have held its form long enough for its magickal purpose.

Biodegradable
Flower Poppet

This is a very pretty poppet and can be fun to make. However, this poppet is more labor intensive than others in this chapter. Sourcing all the ingredients can be tough, but the results are often stunning. As with all biodegradable poppets, it is essential to be mindful of the environment and choose materials that will not harm nature. Florist's foam, wire, rubber bands, and any kind of plastic packaging should be avoided.

Supplies

- Moss or similar biodegradable spongy material
- Twigs or popsicle sticks
- Garden shears or scissors
- Pliable vines, palm or banana leaves, or hemp or jute rope

- Plant-based glue
- Fresh or dried herbs and flowers
- Seeds
- Taglocking items (optional)

Directions

1. Begin by planning the ingredients you'll need. Make a list, then visit your garden, a farmer's market, or your local flower store. Gathering your materials will take time.
2. Cut thirteen or so long strips of vine, palm leaves, or banana leaves using a garden shears or scissors. You may not need them all.
3. Create a lowercase *t* shape with two twigs or popsicle sticks. Alternatively, you can get fancy and create this shape by using two bundles of twigs (tied at the ends and in the middle).
4. Tie the *t* intersection using your long strips, winding them in an *X*-shaped pattern.

5. It's time to bring out some moss or a similarly squishy material. Cut a rectangle of moss the same size as your poppet, then put your *t* shape onto it facedown. Use your strips to tie another *X* shape over the poppet's arms (the horizontal line of the *t* shape). The moss will act as a pocket for stuffing.
6. Use flowers, herbs, and seeds to personalize your poppet. Affix everything to the exterior using biodegradable glue. You could use a daisy, marigold, or rose petal for the face, seeds for eyes, and

thyme or straw for hair. Keep in mind that the colors of your poppet may fade over time, but this adds a touch of personalization.

7. Now, it's time to stuff the poppet with personalizing items like taglocks. Don't overstuff your poppet! Be sure to leave enough space for the poppet to be pliable and easily placed in water or buried.
8. Once the poppet is filled, take an extra-large strip of vine or leaf, secure it around the poppet's waist, and tie a knot. Ensure that the stuffing remains inside.
9. Now that the poppet is closed, you can further enhance your poppet by adding additional items as features or accessories. Secure them using the natural strips or biodegradable glue.
10. Charge your poppet using the directions in chapter 15.

Your poppet is biodegradable and can eventually be disposed of in water, buried, or burned. If you plan to dispose of your poppet by leaving it in water, ensure that it is made from materials that won't harm aquatic life, and consider attaching a stone to the bottom of the poppet to help it sink.

Biodegradable

Beeswax Poppet

This is a fun option if you want to get your hands dirty but you really don't like dirt. There are added benefits to beeswax as well: First, it smells great, and second, your hands will feel smooth afterward.

Supplies

- Modeling beeswax
- Herbs that work with your intent
- Essential oils that work with your intent
- Taglocking items (optional)

Directions

1. Warm your hands and mold the beeswax into the shape of the person the poppet represents, keeping your intention clear in your mind.

2. Rub essential oils that match the intention of the poppet onto the wax. Add herbs that match the intention of the poppet, all the while passionately seeing and imagining the outcome you want.
3. Press taglocking items into the wax if desired.
4. When finished, charge your poppet using the instructions provided in chapter 15.

Keep your poppet in a cool, dry place, preferably sealed in parchment or wax paper. Dust and beeswax are not friends.

Your poppet is biodegradable and can be later disposed of in water, buried, or burned. If you plan to dispose of your poppet by leaving it in water, consider attaching a stone to the bottom of the poppet to help it sink.

Biodegradable
Seed Poppet

This is an easy and fun way to literally grow your magick into flowers in your garden or a planter box.

Supplies

- Seed paper
- Scissors
- A place to plant, such as your garden, a planter box, or a pot
- Taglocking items (optional)
- Plant-based glue (optional)

Directions

1. Cut the seed paper into the shape of the person it is to represent, keeping your intention clear in your mind.
2. Glue taglocking items to the paper if you are using them.
3. Visualize the magick you want to grow. Put the intention into the doll using your voice and breath. Hold the poppet close to your heart, whispering your intentions. For full instructions on charging your poppet, see chapter 15.
4. Plant the seed paper with clear intent. Then, tend to it, water it, and watch it grow.

This kind of poppet will break down in the soil. All you will have left are plants.

Food-Based

French Bread Poppet

This is a tasty way to literally eat your magick. French bread poppets are super easy and fun, yet they are still really powerful. I like to create French bread poppets when I am working health or self-image magick. You can be the target of the spellwork, or you can make a poppet for someone else.

French bread poppets are also fun to do with your coven or a group of friends. It's best if several people make bread poppets for themselves, then everyone eats at the same time. Needless to say, this is a very social way to create a poppet.

Remember, this is the only poppet in the book that is edible.

Supplies

- Large round, uncut loaf of fresh French bread (baked or bought)
- Food coloring for personalization
- Taglocks (optional)

Note: Taglocks are not edible—if you use them, the poppet becomes inedible

Directions

1. If you baked a loaf of French bread from scratch, let it cool.
2. Hold the whole loaf of bread in your hand. Really visualize the magick you want to do and the shifts you (or the person with you) want to make.
3. Feel the hard shell on the outside of the bread. It represents what is blocking you from your desired outcome. Visualize the outcome you want.
4. With clean hands, start digging into the bread gently with your fingers: Open up the shell.
5. When you reach the soft bread inside, start molding it into a human form representing the target while you passionately visualize the desired outcome. The poppet doesn't have to look perfect or detailed—just represent the target of the spellwork.

6. Add words of personalization via food coloring. You can also use food coloring to decorate the poppet.
7. When the poppet is complete, charge it with your intent, words, and breath. See chapter 15 for complete instructions.
8. Time to eat! If you made this poppet for yourself, then consume that magick. If the poppet is for someone else, they get to eat it.

FOOD-BASED

Salt Dough Poppet

Feel like baking? Salt dough poppets can be used for an endless variety of magickal uses. Salt dough can be rolled out and cut into a gingerbread shape with a cookie cutter, or poppets can be shaped by hand. This recipe makes one poppet with some excess dough in case you make any mistakes.

These poppets are inedible. Do not eat them.

Supplies

- 3 cups all-purpose flour, plus flour for your work surface
- 1 cup salt
- Approximately 1 cup water
- Paints or markers to draw on the poppet
- Nonstick baking sheet

- Gingerbread cookie cutter (optional)
- Rolling pin (optional)
- Oven-safe taglocks (optional); inorganic materials like plastics or rubber should not be put in an oven

Directions

1. Preheat the oven to 300 degrees Fahrenheit.
2. Whisk the flour and salt together. Then, gradually stir in the water, creating a dough.
3. Roll the dough out on a floured surface. You can roll it out with a rolling pin or press it by hand.
4. Use a gingerbread cookie cutter to cut the dough into a poppet shape, or shape the figure by hand.
5. Add oven-safe taglocks, if desired.
6. Lay the poppet on a nonstick baking sheet and bake until hard. This will take about an hour.
7. When the poppet has cooled, decorate it with paint or markers. Add sigils, symbols, words, and anything else you feel called to include. Charge the poppet with your intent using the instructions in chapter 15.

This poppet, like other food-based poppets, can be biodegradable if all your ingredients are organic and nontoxic. You may choose to dispose of biodegradable poppets by burying them, burning them, or releasing them in water. If you plan to dispose of your poppet by leaving it in water, consider attaching a stone to the bottom of the poppet to help it sink.

If even one of your ingredients was inorganic, disassemble the poppet to dispose of it. If the dough is too hard to disassemble, soaking your poppet in warm water can help. Then, see chapter 15 for disposal ideas.

FOOD-BASED

Biscuit Poppet

Feel like baking a poppet but hate measuring? Ready-to-bake biscuits are a real option. All it takes is a satisfying pop to open a tube of ready-made dough. The outside of the poppet can be personalized before baking, after baking, or both, depending on the materials used. This recipe makes one poppet.

These poppets are inedible. Do not eat them.

Supplies

- Tube of ready-to-bake biscuits; you can substitute any ready-to-bake dough that does not have to be rolled out, or you can make biscuit dough from scratch if you so choose
- Nonstick baking sheet
- Food coloring, colored sugar, icing, nuts, dried fruit, food paint, etc., for decorating your poppet

- Melon baller, ice cream scoop, or small cup
- Straight edge like that found on a knife, pastry cutter, or spatula
- Herbs that work with your intent
- Essential oils that work with your intent
- Oven-safe taglocking items (optional); stay away from plastics, rubber, and other inorganic items

Directions

1. Follow the manufacturer's instructions and unwrap your dough. If you made your own dough, roll it out. Preheat the oven to the required temperature.
2. Use kitchen tools to shape parts of the figure. I recommend using a small cup or melon baller to shape the head and using a knife, a pastry cutter, or the edge of a spatula to mold the arms, legs, and torso. Remember to make the torso wide enough to incorporate herbs, taglocking items, and other ingredients. You can also use your hands to shape the dough into the person it is to represent, keeping your intention clear in your mind.
3. Arrange your poppet on a nonstick baking sheet. The next step is to take a straight-edged instrument and make an incision down

the center of the poppet's torso. As violent as this seems, it'll look fine after it's baked.

4. In the opening you just created, insert herbs, taglocking items, and other ingredients that match the intention of the poppet. Then, pinch the dough back together.
5. If desired, add drops of aligning essential oils onto the poppet while visualizing the outcome you want.
6. You can incorporate color magick by decorating the poppet to reflect the color that aligns with your intention. Colored sugars and food coloring are good for this.
7. Bake the poppet according to the manufacturer's instructions (or, if you made it yourself, follow the recipe). Don't burn the dough. Remember that underdone poppets are okay, because you're not going to eat these poppets.
8. After removing your puffed-up poppet from the oven, you may choose to do additional decoration like painting or drawing on the poppet with food coloring, paint, or icing. Generally, I find the biscuits are too porous to use ink.
9. When your poppet has cooled, you should be able to hold it close to your heart so you can whisper your intentions into it. There are instructions for charging your poppet in chapter 15. If your

poppet falls apart, toothpicks are your friend! Use them to stick your poppet back together.

10. Store your poppet somewhere safe. This poppet can be kept for a couple of days if you use clear food shellac, a product that keeps store-bought cakes, candy, and apples looking pretty. Please do not use anything other than edible food shellac to add a protective glaze to your poppets, especially if your goal is to bury the poppet or submerge it in water.

This poppet, like other food-based poppets, can be biodegradable if all your ingredients are organic and nontoxic. You may choose to dispose of biodegradable poppets by burying them, burning them, or releasing them in water. If you plan to dispose of your poppet by leaving it in water, consider attaching a stone to the bottom of the poppet to help it sink.

If even one of your ingredients was inorganic, disassemble the poppet to dispose of it. If the dough is too hard to disassemble, soaking your poppet in warm water can help. Then, see chapter 15 for disposal ideas.

SPELL

Prosperity Poppet

Creating a prosperity poppet can be approached in various ways. Prosperity can mean financial abundance, material abundance, or even experiential abundance in any area of life. Maybe you want an opportunity, like a better-paying job, or maybe you're looking for a new home.

Here are my suggested ingredients for a prosperity poppet as well as a spell outline.

Ingredient Options for a Prosperity Poppet

- **Fabric:** Choose green fabric to represent wealth and abundance. Use a small piece of green cloth or felt to create the doll's body, or attach green fabric to your poppet in some way.
- **Stuffing:** Fill the doll with a combination of herbs or materials that are associated with prosperity and abundance. Some options include basil, cinnamon, mint, chamomile, and bay

leaves. These herbs are believed to attract money and financial opportunities.

- **Personal Items:** Include items that symbolize wealth and abundance. You could choose a small coin, a piece of jewelry, a written intention or affirmation related to financial prosperity, or any item that holds significance for you in relation to prosperity.
- **Decorative Elements:** Use green ribbon or embroidery thread to decorate your poppet. You can also add symbols or sigils associated with money and prosperity.

Spell Directions

1. Set your intention. Before starting, take a moment to clearly define your intention for the prosperity poppet. Visualize and affirm the prosperity you desire.
2. Construct the poppet. Create the poppet using green fabric, even if that just means wrapping a green cloth around the poppet. If you are constructing the poppet from fabric, stitch or glue the fabric together, leaving a small opening for stuffing. As you construct the poppet, infuse the doll with your intention to attract prosperity and abundance.
3. Add stuffing and personal items. Fill the doll with your chosen herbs or stuffing materials associated with prosperity. Place

personal items inside the doll, symbolizing your connection to wealth and success.

4. Close and seal the doll. Finish sewing or gluing the doll to seal it. As you do so, envision the doll becoming a magnet for abundance and opportunities.
5. Charge the poppet. Hold the poppet in your hands and visualize vibrant green energy flowing into it. State your intention aloud or silently, affirming your specific desire for prosperity/abundance. You can recite a specific affirmation or chant that resonates with you. If you don't have one, you can just repeat one word associated with your goal, like "Money, money, money, money, money, money ..."
6. Activate the spell. Choose a method to activate the spell. You may place the poppet on your altar, carry it with you in a purse or pocket, or put it in a location associated with prosperity, such as your wallet or in your workspace. Whenever you interact with the poppet, focus on your intention and reinforce your belief in the manifestation of your goals.

Remember, the effectiveness of spells and rituals can vary based on individual beliefs, energy, and intentions. It's important to approach spellwork with respect, focus, and a positive mindset.

Spell

Love Poppet

Creating a love poppet can be a really positive experience. This poppet magick could be for all kinds of love: romantic love, sensual love, friendship, or even self-love.

I do not recommend performing this spell with the goal of ensnaring a specific person into a relationship. This gets into questionable ethics about controlling other people and impeding on their free will. Instead, you could ask for the perfect love. That will give you the best result, whether or not it is the person you are thinking of.

Here are my suggested ingredients for a love poppet as well as a spell outline.

Ingredient Options for a Love Poppet

- **Fabric:** Choose a piece of fabric in a color that symbolizes love or romance, such as pink or red. Use a small piece of cloth or felt to create the doll's body, or attach the fabric to your poppet in some way.

- **Stuffing:** Fill the doll with a combination of herbs or materials that are associated with love. Some options include rose petals, lavender, jasmine, damiana, and hibiscus. These herbs are believed to enhance love, passion, and attraction.
- **Personal Items:** Include items that symbolize love and connection. You could choose a small piece of jewelry, a lock of your hair, a photo, a written intention or affirmation related to love, or any item that holds significance for you in relation to love.
- **Decorative Elements:** Use ribbons, lace, or embroidery thread to decorate your poppet, choosing colors associated with love and romance. You can also add symbols or sigils associated with love.

Spell Directions

1. Set your intention. Before starting, take a moment to clearly define your intention for the love poppet. Visualize and affirm the love, romance, or connection you desire.
2. Construct the poppet. Create the poppet using your chosen material. Stitch or glue the fabric together, leaving a small opening for

stuffing. As you construct the poppet, infuse the doll with your intention to attract love or romantic connection.

3. Add stuffing and personal items. Fill the doll with your chosen herbs or stuffing materials associated with love. Place personal items inside the doll, symbolizing your connection to love.
4. Close and seal the doll. Finish sewing or gluing the doll to seal it. As you do so, visualize the doll becoming a magnet for love, passion, or romantic opportunities.
5. Charge the poppet. Hold the poppet in your hands and visualize vibrant, loving energy flowing into it. State your intention aloud or silently, affirming your specific desire for love or romantic connection. You can recite a specific affirmation or chant that resonates with you. If you don't have one, you can just repeat one word associated with your goal, like "Romance, romance, romance, romance, romance, romance …"
6. Activate the spell. Choose a method to activate the spell. You may place the poppet on your altar, keep it under your pillow, or put it in a location associated with love, such as your bedroom. Whenever you interact with the poppet, focus on your intention and reinforce your belief in the manifestation of love.

Remember, the effectiveness of spells and rituals can vary based on individual beliefs, energy, and intentions. It's important to approach spell-work with respect, focus, and a positive mindset. Additionally, keep in mind that the spell should be used to attract genuine love and connection; it's crucial to respect the free will and consent of others.

Spell

Healing Poppet

A healing poppet can be intended for physical, emotional, or even spiritual healing. I've performed this beautiful spell countless times, for everything from heartache to hospital stays. A healing poppet can be directed at another person or at yourself. As with all poppet spell-work involving other people, you should get their consent. If that person cannot give their consent, reach out to them energetically and ask their permission. Your intuition will tell you if they consent.

Here are my suggested ingredients for a healing poppet as well as a spell outline.

Ingredient Options for a Healing Poppet

- **Fabric:** Choose a color that resonates with healing and well-being, such as light blue or green. Use a small piece of cloth or felt to create the doll's body, or attach the fabric to your poppet in some way.

- **Stuffing:** Fill the doll with a combination of herbs or materials that are associated with healing and health. Some options include lavender, chamomile, rosemary, eucalyptus, and sage. These herbs are believed to promote physical, emotional, and spiritual healing.
- **Personal Items:** Include items that symbolize healing and restoration. You could choose a small crystal, a written intention or affirmation related to healing, a lock of hair, or any item that holds significance for you in relation to healing.
- **Decorative Elements:** Use ribbons, embroidery thread, or symbols associated with healing to decorate your poppet. You could incorporate the caduceus, a universal healing symbol, or any other symbol that resonates with you.

Spell Directions

1. Set your intention. Before starting, take a moment to clearly define your intention for the healing poppet. Visualize and affirm the healing, well-being, and restoration you desire.
2. Construct the poppet. Create the poppet using your chosen material. Stitch or glue the fabric together, leaving a small opening for

stuffing. As you construct the poppet, infuse the doll with your intention for healing and wellness.

3. Add the stuffing and personal items. Fill the doll with your chosen herbs or stuffing materials associated with healing. Place personal items inside the doll, symbolizing your connection to healing and restoration.
4. Close and seal the doll. Finish sewing or gluing the doll to seal it. As you do so, visualize the doll becoming a vessel of healing energy, supporting your intention for physical, emotional, or spiritual healing.
5. Charge the poppet. Hold the poppet in your hands and visualize radiant, healing energy flowing into it. State your intention aloud or silently, affirming your specific desire for healing and well-being. You can recite a specific affirmation or chant that resonates with you. If you don't have one, you can just repeat one word associated with your goal, like "Health, health, health, health, health, health …"
6. Activate the spell. Choose a method to activate the spell. You may place the poppet on your altar, keep it near your bedside, or hold it during healing meditations. Whenever you interact with the poppet, focus on your intention and reinforce your belief in the manifestation of your goals.

Remember, the effectiveness of spells and rituals can vary based on individual beliefs, energy, and intentions. It's important to approach spellwork with respect, focus, and a positive mindset. Additionally, remember that a healing poppet is not a substitute for professional medical care. Magick should be used as a complementary practice to support your well-being.

Spell

Binding Poppet

Binding poppets can be very useful. A binding spell energetically binds your target from being able to hurt you in any way. Binding poppets can be used to bind someone from doing anything negative to you, such as spreading rumors about you. However, ethical consideration is very important if you are binding someone. If your goal goes beyond defensive magick, you are venturing into the darker areas of spellcraft, so be very careful with your intent. The goal is to defend yourself, not to harm the person you are binding. When used defensively, binding poppets can be very empowering.

Here are my suggested ingredients for a binding poppet as well as a spell outline.

Ingredient Options for a Binding Poppet

- **Fabric:** Choose a color that represents protection and containment, such as black or dark purple. Use a small piece of cloth or felt to create the doll's body, or attach the fabric to your poppet in some way.
- **Stuffing:** Fill the doll with a combination of herbs or materials that are associated with protection and warding off negative energies. Some options include rosemary, sage, lavender, black salt, and St. John's wort. You can also choose a stone like black tourmaline, which will dispel negative energy while attracting positive energy.
- **Personal Items:** Include items that represent the person or situation you wish to bind. You could choose a photograph, a name written on a scrap of paper, or any item that holds significance for you in relation to the person or situation.
- **Sigils and Symbols:** You may choose to draw a protective sigil or symbol, such as the Helm of Awe.
- **Binding Materials:** Select items that symbolize binding or containment. These will be used to wrap and bind the poppet. You could choose black thread, black ribbon, or twine, for example.

Spell Directions

1. Set your intention. Before starting, clearly define your intention for the binding poppet. Determine the specific person, situation, or energy you wish to bind. Visualize and affirm your intention for containment and protection.
2. Construct the poppet. Create the poppet using the chosen fabric. Stitch or glue the fabric together, leaving a small opening for stuffing. As you construct the poppet, focus on infusing the doll with your intention for binding and containment.
3. Add the binding materials, stuffing, and personal items. Place some of the binding materials, such as black thread or ribbon, inside the doll. Fill the doll with your chosen herbs or stuffing materials associated with protection. Place personal items inside the doll, including items that represent the person or situation you wish to bind. You could choose a photograph, a name written on a scrap of paper, or any symbolic object.
4. Close and seal the doll. Finish sewing or gluing the doll to seal it. As you do so, visualize the poppet becoming a vessel for containment and protection, forming a shield around the targeted person or situation.

5. Bind the poppet. Take the remaining black thread or ribbon and wrap it around the doll's body, symbolizing the binding and containment of the targeted person or energy. As you bind the poppet, recite a specific affirmation or chant that reflects your intention.
6. Charge the poppet. Hold the poppet in your hands and visualize a powerful shield forming around the person or situation you wish to bind. State your intention aloud or silently, affirming the effectiveness of the binding and the protection it provides. You can recite a specific affirmation or chant that resonates with you. You need to feel it in every cell of your body, every thought in your head, every word uttered. Speak a phrase that will make this intention reality. You have the power.
7. Activate the spell. Choose a method to activate the spell. You may place the poppet on your altar, bury it in the ground, or keep it in a secure location. Whenever you interact with the poppet, focus on reinforcing the binding and containment, maintaining a strong intention for protection.

Remember, the effectiveness of spells and rituals can vary based on individual beliefs, energy, and intentions. It's important to approach spellwork with respect, focus, and a positive mindset. Additionally, consider the ethics and consequences of binding spells, as they involve influencing the free will and actions of others. Use binding spells responsibly. Consider alternative methods of resolving conflict or protecting yourself when possible.

Spell

Protection Poppet

Protection poppets can be created for yourself, your children, or even your pets! This is a very versatile spell. A protection poppet can be purposed as a spell for general well-being or for something specific. For example, I have used protection poppets when dealing with particularly cursed haunted dolls.

Here are my suggested ingredients for a protection poppet as well as a spell outline.

Ingredient Options for a Protection Poppet

- **Fabric:** Choose a color that represents protection and security, such as white, silver, or blue. Use a small piece of cloth or felt to create the doll's body, or attach the fabric to your poppet in some way.

- **Stuffing:** Fill the doll with a combination of herbs or materials that are associated with protection and warding off negative energies. Some options include rosemary, basil, sage, lavender, and bay leaves.
- **Personal Items:** Include items that symbolize protection to you. You could choose a small amulet, a charm, a talisman, or any object that holds significance for you in relation to protection.
- **Sigils and Symbols:** You may choose to draw a sigil or symbol, or even a word or emoji that speaks to your intent.
- **Crystals and Stones:** Choose protective crystals and stones that resonate with you, such as black tourmaline, obsidian, amethyst, and clear quartz. These stones are believed to repel negative energies and enhance protective vibrations.

Spell Directions

1. Set your intention. Before starting, take a moment to clearly define your intention for the protection poppet. Visualize and affirm a shield of protection surrounding you or the person for whom you're creating the poppet. Focus on the specific areas or aspects you wish to protect.
2. Construct the poppet. Create the poppet using your chosen material. Stitch or glue the fabric together, leaving a small opening for

stuffing. As you construct the poppet, infuse the doll with your intention for protection, envisioning the poppet as a powerful guardian.

3. Add stuffing, personal items, and crystals. Fill the doll with your chosen herbs and crystals. Place personal items inside the doll, symbolizing your connection to protection. Visualize the items' energy infusing the poppet and amplifying its protective qualities.
4. Close and seal the doll. Finish sewing or gluing the doll to seal it. As you do so, visualize the poppet becoming a powerful shield, providing a protective barrier against negative energies and influences.
5. Charge the poppet. Hold the poppet in your hands and visualize a glowing, protective energy enveloping it. State your intention aloud or silently, affirming the effectiveness of the poppet as a guardian and protector. You can recite a specific affirmation or chant that resonates with you. If you don't have one, you can just repeat one word associated with your goal, like "Protection, protection, protection, protection, protection, protection ..."
6. Activate the spell. Choose a method to activate the spell. You may place the poppet on your altar, keep it near your bedside, or carry it with you as a personal talisman. Whenever you interact with

the poppet, focus on reinforcing its protective energy, maintaining a strong intention for safety and well-being.

Remember, the effectiveness of spells and rituals can vary based on individual beliefs, energy, and intentions. It's important to approach spellwork with respect, focus, and a positive mindset.

Conclusion

As we reach the conclusion of this exploration into the realm of poppets and haunted dolls, I find myself filled with gratitude and a sense of deep fulfillment. Throughout this book, I have shared the remarkable power of intention, the art of creating sacred vessels, and the profound interconnectedness of the physical and spiritual realms. Yet, amidst the spells and rituals, what truly shines is the universal message of love, healing, and empowerment that runs through every thread and every heartfelt intention embedded in these humble creations.

May this book serve as a guiding beacon for all those who seek to tap into the ancient wisdom of poppets, igniting their own innate magick and fostering a world brimming with harmony, compassion, and awe. As we bid farewell, let us carry the magick of poppets within us, forever transformed and forever linked to the boundless potential residing within.

Blessed be.

Bibliography

American Psychiatric Association. *Diagnostic and Statistical Manual of Mental Disorders*. 5th ed. American Psychiatric Association Publishing, 2013.

Atwal, Sanj. "The Haunting Story of the Man Who Built the Island of the Dolls." Guinness World Records, October 26, 2022. https://www.guinnessworldrecords.com/news/2022/10/the-haunting-story-of-the-man-who-built-the-island-of-dolls-723402.

Baser, K. Husnu Can, Ayten Altintas, and Mine Kurkcuoglu. "Turkish Rose: A Review of the History, Ethnobotany, and Modern Uses of Rose Petals, Rose Oil, Rose Water, and Other Rose Products." *HerbalGram* 96 (2012): 40–53.

Beall, Rachel. "Mugwort." Washington College. Accessed January 21, 2025. https://www.washcoll.edu/learn-by-doing/lifelong-learning/plants/asteraceae/artemisia-vulgaris.php.

Bird-David, Nurit. "'Animism' Revisted: Personhood, Environment, and Relational Epistemology." *Current Anthropology* 40, no. S1 (1999). https://www.journals.uchicago.edu/doi/10.1086/200061.

Brixius, Dorit. "A Hard Nut to Crack: Nutmeg Cultivation and the Application of Natural History Between the Maluku Islands and Isle de

France (1750s–1780s)." *The British Journal for the History of Science* 51, no. 4 (2018): 585–606. https://doi.org/10.1017/S0007087418000754.

Calder, Ruth. "Plant 327." University of Oxford. Accessed December 5, 2024. https://herbaria.plants.ox.ac.uk/bol/plants400/Profiles/op/Ocimum.

"Calendula." MedlinePlus. Updated June 20, 2023. https://medlineplus.gov/druginfo/natural/235.html.

Carter-Lome, Maxine. "The Evolution of Mourning Wear." The Journal of Antiques and Collectibles, October 4, 2022. https://journalofantiques.com/features/the-evolution-of-mourning-wear.

Cave, James. "So What Exactly Is Allspice, Anyway?" *Huffpost*, December 16, 2015. https://www.huffpost.com/entry/what-is-allspice_n_5671b849e4b0dfd4bcc044e9.

Chen, Gang, Salma Mostafa, Zhaogeng Lu, Ran Du, Jiawen Cui, Yun Wang, Qinggang Liao, Jinkai Lu, Xinyu Mao, Bang Chang, Quan Gan, Li Wang, Zhichao Jia, Xiulian Yang, Yingfang Zhu, Jianbin Yan, and Biao Jin. "The Jasmine (Jasminum sambac) Genome Provides Insight into the Biosynthesis of Flower Fragrances and Jasmonates." *Genomics Proteomics Bioinformatics* 21, no. 1 (2023). https://www.doi.org/10.1016/j.gpb.2022.12.005.

"Clove." History and Special Collections, UCLA Louise M. Darling Biomedical Library. Accessed December 5, 2024. https://unitproj.library.ucla.edu/biomed/spice/index.cfm?displayID=7.

Collén, Jonas, M. Lynn Cornish, James Craigie, Elizabeth Ficko-Blean, Cécile Hervé, Stacy A. Krueger-Hadfield, Catherine Leblanc, Gurvan Michel, Philippe Potin, Thierry Tonon, and Catherine Boyen. "Chapter Three – *Chondrus crispus* – A Present and Historical Model Organism for Red Seaweeds." *Advances in Botanical Research* 71 (2014): 53–89. https://doi.org/10.1016/B978-0-12-408062-1.00003-2.

Cook, Jill. "The Lion Man: An Ice Age Masterpiece." The British Museum, October 10, 2017. https://www.britishmuseum.org/blog/lion-man-ice-age-masterpiece.

Corley, Brianna. "The Specific Cinnamon Variety That Makes Cinnabon So Delicious." Daily Meal, January 23, 2023. https://www.thedailymeal.com/1175456/the-specific-cinnamon-variety-that-makes-cinnabon-so-delicious/.

Daryaee, Touraj. "The Scent of Musk and Jasmine: Trade in Aromatics Between Iran and China." *ḴORĀSĀN-NĀMAK* (2022): 67–74.

Dean, Sam. "The Etymology of Basil." Bon Appétit, June 7, 2013. https://www.bonappetit.com/test-kitchen/ingredients/article/the-etymology-of-basil.

Dickie, Matthew W. "What Is a *Kolossos* and How Were *Kolossoi* Made in the Hellenistic Period?" *Greek, Roman, and Byzantine Studies* 37, no. 3 (1996): 237–40.

Eidell, Lynsey. "The Real-Life Story Behind Annabelle Is Even More Bone-Chilling Than the Movie." *Glamour*, October 7, 2014. https://www.glamour.com/story/real-story-behind-annabelle.

"Essential Oil of Patchouli." American College of Healthcare Sciences. Accessed December 5, 2024. https://files.achs.edu/mediabank/files/achs_patchouli_monograph.pdf.

Ferris, Taylor. "Connecting the Mind and Body in Ancient Greek Medicine." Honors thesis, University of Mississippi, 2018. https://egrove.olemiss.edu/cgi/viewcontent.cgi?article=1898&context=hon_thesis.

Garcia-Fenech, Giovanni. "Day of the Dead, Halloween, and the Scary Side of Artstor." *JSTOR* (blog), October 21, 2011. https://about.jstor.org/blog/day-of-the-dead-halloween-and-the-scary-side-of-artstor/.

Giblin, Elizabeth. "Kewpie Doll Charm Nears the Century Mark." Recordnet, November 21, 2008. https://www.recordnet.com/story/lifestyle/2008/11/22/kewpie-doll-charm-nears-century/52188395007.

Glencairn Museum News. "Sculpting the Afterlife: A Ka Statue at Glencairn Museum." Glencairn Museum, July 11, 2024. https://www

.glencairnmuseum.org/newsletter/2024/7/9/sculpting-the-afterlife-a-ka-statue-at-glencairn-museum.

Grieve, Margaret. *A Modern Herbal*. Vol. 1. Dover Publications, 2013.

Harris, Shawnya L., and Peri Klemm. "Power Figure (*Nkisi Nkondi*), Kongo Peoples." Smart History, August 9, 2015. https://smarthistory.org/nkisi-nkondi-kongo-people/.

Hart, Maria Teresa. "How Porcelain Dolls Became the Ultimate Victorian Status Symbol." *Smithsonian Magazine*, November 1, 2022. https://www.smithsonianmag.com/history/how-porcelain-dolls-became-the-ultimate-status-symbol-180980945.

"History of Lavender." Cache Creek Lavender. Accessed October 29, 2024. https://www.cachecreeklavender.com/history-of-lavender.html.

Hosmer, Herbert H., Jr. "Hand-Made and Home-Made American Paper Dolls." Edited by Janet R. Macfarlane. *New York History* 33, no. 4 (1952): 438–47. https://www.jstor.org/stable/23153601.

Hyland, David C. "The Well-Dressed Venus: Women's Wear ca. 27,000 BP." *Archaeology, Ethnology, and Anthropology of Eurasia* 1, no. 1 (2000): 2–21. https://www.researchgate.net/publication/271853486_The_Well-Dressed_Venus_Women's_Wear_ca_27000_BP.

Idel, Moshe. *Golem: Jewish Magical and Mystical Traditions on the Artificial Anthropoid*. State University of New York Press, 1990.

Jayaraman, Ilamathi. "Health Benefits Uses of Black Salt." *Research and Reviews in Biotechnology and Biosciences* 9, no. 2 (2022): 41–46. https://doi.org/10.5281/zenodo.7932924.

LaGamma, Alisa. *Kongo: Power and Majesty*. The Metropolitan Museum of Art, 2015.

Lanese, Nicoletta. "Traces of an Ancient Human Culture from 40,000 Years Ago Unearthed in China." *ScienceAlert*, March 2, 2022. https://www.sciencealert.com/stunning-new-example-of-anceint-stone-age-culture-unearthed-in-northern-china.

McLoughin, Pam. "Real 'Annabelle' Story Shared by Lorraine Warren at Milford's Lauralton Hall." *New Haven Register*, October 4, 2014. https://www.nhregister.com/living/article/Real-Annabelle-story-shared-by-Lorraine-11382545.php.

Mérida-Reyes, Max Samuel, Manuel Alejandro Muñoz-Wug, Bessie Evelyn Oliva-Hernández, Isabel Cristina Gaitán-Fernández, Daniel Luiz Reis Simas, Antonio Jorge Ribeiro da Silva, and Juan Francisco Pérez-Sabino. "Composition and Antibacterial Activity of the Essential Oil from Pimenta dioica (L.) Merr. from Guatemala." *Medicines* 7, no. 10 (2020). https://www.doi.org/10.3390/medicines7100059.

Miller, Maggie. "Paranormal Playthings: The World's Most Famous Haunted Dolls." Accessed October 10, 2024. https://www.travel

channel.com/ghostober/articles/paranormal-playthings-the-worlds-most-famous-haunted-dolls.

"Miscellany." *Swindle & Fraud* 8, no. 2 (2015).

Mrad, Selima Ben. "Spice Trade: A History of a Fantasy Substance." *CHARM* (2005): 11–15.

Murugan, Ramar, and C. Livingstone. "Origin of the Name 'Patchouli' and Its History." *Current Science* 99, no. 9 (2010): 1274–76.

Negri, Patti, host. *The Witching Hour*. "Scared & Alone with Robert the Doll and David L. Sloan." June 20, 2022. https://witchinghourpodcast.podbean.com/e/scared-alone-with-robert-the-doll-and-david-lsloan/.

Pearlstone, Zena. "Brian Honyouti: Send in the Clowns." *American Indian Culture and Research Journal* 36, no. 3 (2012): 45–73.

Pincus, Donna. "Fears, Phobias, and Anxiety." The Child Anxiety Network. Accessed October 10, 2024. http://www.childanxiety.net/Fears_Phobias_Anxiety.htm.

Podhajny, Richard M. "History, Shellfish, Royalty, and the Color People." *Paper, Film & Foil Converter*, July 1, 2002. https://pffc-online.com/ar/1348-paper-history-shellfish-royalty.

Rait, Satwant. "Sikh Mourning." *Living with Dying* (blog), June 25, 2018. https://livingwithdying.leeds.ac.uk/2018/06/25/sikh-mourning/.

Reider, Noriko T. "Tsukumogami ki 付喪神記 (The Record of Tool Specters)." *Japanese Journal of Religious Studies* 36, no. 2 (2009): 1–19. https://nirc.nanzan-u.ac.jp/journal/6/issue/179/article/1275.

"Rosemary for Remembrance." The Solidago School of Herbalism, January 23, 2021. https://www.solidagoherbschool.com/blog/2021/1/23/rosemary-for-remembrance.

Sandborn, Dixie. "Plant Science at the Dinner Table: Peppermint." Michigan State University, December 1, 2021. https://www.canr.msu.edu/news/peppermint-and-the-science-behind-it.

"'Scapegoat Doll' May Have Blended Shinto, Buddhist Rites." *Archaeology Magazine*, March 29, 2018. https://archaeology.org/news/2018/03/29/180329-japan-wooden-hitogata/.

Shakespeare, William. *Hamlet*. Edited by Barbara Mowat, Paul Werstine, Michael Poston, and Rebecca Niles. Folger Shakespeare Library. https://www.folger.edu/explore/shakespeares-works/hamlet/read/4/5/.

Shakespeare, William. *The Tragedy of Romeo and Juliet*. Edited by Barbara Mowat, Paul Werstine, Michael Poston, and Rebecca Niles. Folger Shakespeare Library. https://www.folger.edu/explore/shakespeares-works/romeo-and-juliet/read/2/2/.

Streit, Katharina. "A Maximalist Interpretation of the Execration Texts—Archaeological and Historical Implications of a High Chronology."

Journal of Ancient Egyptian Interconnections 13 (March 2017): 59–69. https://www.academia.edu/31674906/Streit_K_2017_A_Maximalist_Interpretation_of_the_Execration_Texts_Archaeological_and_Historical_Implications_of_a_High_Chronology_Journal_of_Ancient_Egyptian_Interconnections_13_59_69.

Swamy, Mallappa Kumara, and Uma Rani Sinniah. "A Comprehensive Review on the Phytochemical Constituents and Pharmacological Activities of *Pogostemon cablin* Benth.: An Aromatic Medicinal Plant of Industrial Importance." *Molecules* 20, no. 5 (2015). https://doi.org/10.3390/molecules20058521.

"Testimonials & Apologies." Robert the Doll. Accessed December 5, 2024. https://robertthedoll.org/letters/.

"Want to Seek Goddess Durga's Blessings? Follow These Rituals During Navratri." *News 18*. Updated October 8, 2023. https://www.news18.com/lifestyle/want-to-seek-goddess-durgas-blessings-follow-these-rituals-during-navratri-8607517.html.

Wright, Barton. "Hopi Kachinas: A Life Force." In *Hopi Nation: Essays on Indigenous Art, Culture, History, and Law*, edited by Edna Glenn, John R. Wunder, Willard Hughes Rollings, and C. L. Martin. University of Nebraska–Lincoln, 2008.

Zaouali, Lilia. *Medieval Cuisine of the Islamic World: A Concise History with 174 Recipes*. Translated by M. B. DeBevoise. University of California Press, 2009.

To Write to the Author

If you wish to contact the author or would like more information about this book, please write to the author in care of Llewellyn Worldwide Ltd. and we will forward your request. Both the author and publisher appreciate hearing from you and learning of your enjoyment of this book and how it has helped you. Llewellyn Worldwide Ltd. cannot guarantee that every letter written to the author can be answered, but all will be forwarded. Please write to:

Patti Negri
℅ Llewellyn Worldwide
2143 Wooddale Drive
Woodbury, MN 55125-2989

Please enclose a self-addressed stamped envelope for reply, or $1.00 to cover costs. If outside the U.S.A., enclose an international postal reply coupon.

Many of Llewellyn's authors have websites with additional information and resources. For more information, please visit our website at http://www.llewellyn.com.